THE DAYS
OF WINE AND
SOFTWARE

THE DAYS
OF WINE AND
SOFTWARE

Building a Business
by Following the Principles
of Nature

Dana E. Bruttig

Elfin Cove Press
Seattle, Washington

ELFIN COVE PRESS
914 Virginia St.
Seattle, WA 98101

Project manager: Bernie Kuntz
Cover design: David Marty
Editing and text design: Laurel Strand

Library of Congress 98-074121

ISBN 0944958-39-7

Printed in the United States of America
1   3   5   7   9   10   8   6   4   2

DEDICATION

To Chris Colburn,
For giving me a sunflower,
a tuna sandwich,
a 7 UP,
and my soul.
And for always *telling me the truth.*
Captura is not *a fruit stand.*

And to Barbara Fagan,
for giving me a compass,
a map,
and a place to call home.
And for always believing in me.
Captura is not *just another company.*

And to both of you,
for showing me what it means to be loved,
unconditionally.
It has made all the difference.

CONTENTS

PREFACE
WINE AND SOFTWARE?

THIS BOOK IS about wine and about software, but mostly it is about being an entrepreneur. Written by an entrepreneur for entrepreneurs, it is about risking everything in pursuit of your dreams.

I hope to share the business wisdom that I learned from building my own company based upon time-honored principles and from watching my husband build his vineyard by following the same principles. Vineyard parables are as old as the Bible and yet still applicable in the information age of the 1990s.

In 1994, my husband Christopher and I embarked simultaneously on personal journeys toward self-actualization. We took what appeared to be very different roads — he in the wine industry and myself in the software industry.

As our paths twisted and turned through the years, it became apparent that we were really on the same road. When I came home one day from a brutal round of venture capital meetings to find him fighting an equally brutal drip system in our vineyard, I began noticing the parallels. And when, at long last, I had a product to sell to customers, it was no coincidence that he was pulling in his first harvest.

My company, Captura Software, Inc., creates a product that is used to automate travel and entertainment (T&E) expense reporting. It started with an idea and a handful of people, and now is used by companies such as Merrill Lynch & Co., Aetna Insurance, and Compaq Computers.

Christopher's business, Bruttig Vineyards, produces Syrah and Viognier grapes for use in premium varietal wines. He currently sells his crop to Geyser Peak Winery, produces a small amount under his own label, and hopes to own and operate his own winery within the next few years.

It is my hope that you will find this book useful in assisting you on your entrepreneurial journey as you build your own business. I have designed it to be as interactive as possible, with space for you to jot thoughts and notes about your own business at the end of each section. I have also suggested actions that will assist you in building your business.

I have also tried to teach you a bit about my passion — software — and my husband's passion — wine.

INTRODUCTION

IN SEPTEMBER OF 1993, I was feeling pretty good about life. I was a vice president with a successful software company which had gone public the year before, I was building call centers all over the world, and I was working the requisite hundred-hour weeks so common in my field. I had finally carved out a day to meet my husband in Montana so that I could see the 25 acres we had purchased six months earlier. We both dreamed of the "country life" and, having obtained some extra money via my stock options, we thought Montana was a good place to start realizing our dream.

After spending a day viewing the property, I dropped off my husband in eastern Montana where he was to spend a week elk-hunting. My itinerary had me heading to Denver on business. I was scheduled to take a 7:00 a.m. flight out of Great Falls on Sunday. After squeezing in some solo hiking in Glacier National Park, I awoke at 3:00 a.m. and headed down the cold mountain roads toward the airport, fully expecting to resume my hectic lifestyle. Instead, the path of my life was altered forever.

Somewhere on the highway through the Blackfeet

Indian Reservation, I came around a bend and saw two eyes in the darkness, which instinct told me to avoid. As I slammed hard on the brakes, I felt the car go out of control, spin around, and head backwards into a ten-foot-deep ditch. As the car rolled and rolled, I remember thinking before I blacked out that these were the final moments of my life.

When I regained consciousness, the car was upside down, all the windows were smashed, and I was pinned in my seat. Somehow, I got out of the seatbelt, scrambled out the back window, and climbed to the road. I stood there looking down at the totaled automobile, feeling no pain at all, and concluded that I must be dead, because I could not possibly have survived such a wreck without injury. Because nothing like this had ever happened to me before, I did not realize that I was in shock, which makes it possible to be severely injured without knowing it. It only seemed logical that I must be dead. To confirm this, I went back down to the car to find my body. I must have wandered for ten or fifteen minutes before first feeling significant pain. As soon as the pain began, I lay down next to the car in the pitch-black darkness and knew two things: one, I was alive and, two, I would surely die from internal injuries or exposure.

I lay there for what seemed to be hours, but which was probably only thirty minutes or so. I thought of my three children who did not really know me, of all the secrets from my childhood that had affected my life, of my workaholism and its impact on all my relationships. I made a lot of vows beside that deserted road in Montana.

Out of the darkness, I saw car headlights. In the car were two Native Americans on their way to work at the reservation medical center. They picked me up, kept me warm, and got me the help I needed. It took me three months to recover, during which time I experienced major depression and started on a path of self-rediscovery. When I returned to work, the company was in turmoil, the executive staff had been removed, and new management was in place. I looked at my bank balance, decided I had more than enough money, and took my cue to exit.

At the same time, my husband was re-evaluating his career path. He had been employed within the penal system, first as a probation counselor working with juveniles and then as a lay chaplain working with adult males in the Los Angeles County jail. He was ready to make a change. As a young man in college, he had worked with his father in founding the Franciscan

Winery in Napa, California. That experience gave him a passion for wine and winemaking that had never left him. Because entering the wine industry required large amounts of capital and working in the wine industry did not pay as well as his current profession, he had never considered re-entering the world of wine.

In that summer of 1994, we both decided to pursue our dreams. We were in the enviable position of having enough money (or so we thought) to do so. We relocated our family to the heart of the wine country in Sonoma County, where Christopher could plant his vineyard and I could pursue my dream of being with my children in a small-town environment.

Soon after we made the move, I got a phone call from Gerald, my former CEO and mentor, who was then living in Florida. He was wondering what I was up to, and we agreed to meet for lunch while we were both in Los Angeles and catch up on each other's doings.

By way of introduction, Gerald is the person who modeled for me what an entrepreneur is. He spent ten years building a successful software company and is a brilliant visionary who can enlist others in making his dream happen. When his blue eyes sparkle and his ears wiggle and he says, "I've been thinking," anyone around becomes mesmerized.

Over lunch back in 1994, our conversation began innocently enough:

Gerald said, "You know, Dana, I've been thinking — what if there were a way to solve the expense-reporting nightmare for corporations? Don't you think that would be a huge market?"

I responded, "Yes, I do. In fact, almost every one of our customers asked about it."

Gerald then said, "This company I'm running has a human resources system that runs on a rules engine. I think if *we* [notice how slyly this entered the conversation] used the same approach, *we* could truly capture all the data necessary to really automate T&E."

"Workflow for T&E? Tell me more."

The hook set and my interest piqued, Gerald began to reel me in. "Yes, workflow. See, most companies have no idea how much they're spending, who is approving expenses, or which department should be charged for the expense. It was always one of my biggest frustrations as a CEO."

With heightened interest, I said, "How long do you think it would take to build an application like that?"

Gerald responded (and I am *not* making this up), "Oh, it would be so easy, six months with the right people, maybe a year tops."

Immediately, I saw an opportunity. I thought to myself, "Gerald has a proven track record in seeing a market way ahead of time. I have some money still in savings that I was going to use to start my consulting business. Maybe I should just invest it in a business."

I said, "Gerald, this sounds like a great idea. How much do you think it would cost to get through that first six to twelve months?"

Gerald, with a straight face, said, "I would guess a few guys, plus office rent — keep expenses down — maybe $250,000."

And that was how it started. Within a few weeks and a few more conversations, I was fully enrolled in the concept for my new business and had even expanded it to include the kind of company it would be, the kind of people who would work there, and the kind of customer delight we would create.

Over the next three years, I built the company, ran the company (headquartered in Seattle, Washington) and earned the right to call myself CEO, president, and chairman. It took two years and $2.5 million to get that "six-month, $250,000" product to market. It has been quite a journey, filled with fun and learning, but also with pain and despair.

What follows are the lessons that I learned along

the way and the principles I encourage you to follow, should you decide to take the same road.

As the English philosopher John Ruskin said, "The reward for our toil is not what we get from it, but what we become by it."

THE
POWER
OF
PASSION

Only passions, great
passions, can elevate the
soul to great things.
— Denis Diderot

CLIMATE AND SOIL

CREATING GOOD WINE starts with the grapes, and producing high-quality grapes starts with the climate and the soil.

Grapes are native to the warm, temperate latitudes between 34°N and 49°S. The areas designated as "wine country" throughout the world tend to fall within this zone and have similar climates. Of course, wine grapes are grown farther north and south, but they are cultivated most successfully in those areas, such as France and California, that are located within this temperate zone.

Equally important as the climate is the soil. Grapes are deeply rooted plants, sending their roots six feet down or more, so a vineyard site must have adequate topsoil and drainage.

Once you know which kind of grape you want to plant, you must find the proper soil and climate for that variety. Vines planted as little as 100 yards apart can produce entirely different wines. In addition, each grape has particular characteristics that can be enhanced by a particular location. For example, Pinot Noir does well on slopes, while Chardonnay prefers valley floors. When the climate and soil are a perfect match for the varietal, you have a reasonable chance of producing good wine.

The same fundamentals hold true for entrepreneurs. Our "climate" is the entrepreneurial spirit that drives us to believe in the so-called impossible, and our "soil" is a unique blend of passion and vision. Think of the great entrepreneurs you have known or admired — Henry Ford, Sam Walton, Bill Gates. These men all had passion and vision in abundance combined with exceptional belief in themselves, and they used those basic ingredients to change the world.

Fundamentally, I believe that is what it means to be an entrepreneur: we are the dreamers of dreams who make new things possible. Our ability to dream, along with our passion and vision, creates the perfect environment — the perfect climate and soil — that allows ideas to flourish. In some way, however large or small, we leave the world a different place than we found it.

THE PROPER CLIMATE
—∿—
THE ENTREPRENEURIAL MINDSET

I was raised in classic 1950s suburbia. My father worked as a corporate manager, and my mother was a housewife. I was the middle of three children. We were encouraged to do well in school, respect authority, and be "good kids."

My mother was not very attentive to us as young children, so my older brother and I spent lots of time on our own exploring the local parks and shops and creating a world of our own. That was when I first exercised my "entrepreneurial" muscles. At the ages of six and four, we were enterprising in figuring out how to meet our basic needs. For lunch, we either attended the "sample give-away" days at different grocery stores or we collected and returned bottles for change, which we then used to rig the vending machines to dispense several candies at once.

Of course, it was not until many years later that I learned the definition of the word "entrepreneur." As a child, I only knew that it was a long word which my father often said with contempt. I knew it was some kind of profession because it was always mentioned during discussions of what some person or another did for a living. Based on the tone of voice my father used, I knew it was not something I wanted to be when I grew up.

Because this is a book by an entrepreneur for entrepreneurs, I think it is only fair that, before you read further, we should be clear about what an entrepreneur really is. With all due respect to my father, entrepreneurship is not a profession to disdain. On the contrary, it is one of the noblest of callings. It is one of the very few professions that can change the world.

But what does the word really mean? Webster defines it as "a person who organizes and manages a business undertaking, assuming the risk for the sake of the profit."

I think you will find the current popular definition to be a bit different. Whenever I ask people what they think "entrepreneur" means, their responses always include the words "innovation," "creativity," or "vision." In fact, I believe most people think of "inventor" or "leader" when they hear the word "entrepreneur."

By contrast, Webster defines "leader" as "a person that leads; directing, commanding, or guiding head, as of a group or activity."

Very different definitions, aren't they? While there are many books that will help you learn to become a better leader, those skills are not the ones that will lead to your success as an entrepreneur. What you hold in your hands now, though, is a book that will help you identify and strengthen the unique skills necessary for your success as your own boss.

The prerequisite to being an entrepreneur is that you were born with, or developed along the way, what I call "the entrepreneurial mindset." This is the set of beliefs that propels you into taking on the task of organizing a business undertaking and assuming the risk. The attributes that determine whether you are in the right "climate zone" to be an entrepreneur are:

- You have an unshakable belief in yourself.
- You see things as they could be instead of how they are.
- You can handle ambiguity; you embrace the unknown.
- You believe that there are always multiple solutions to any one problem.
- You always see the possibilities in any situation.
- You can be so persuasive that people have a hard time saying no to you.
- You are doggedly determined; you never give up.

- You have an overabundance of physical and mental energy.
- You are enthusiastic.
- You believe in the potential of others.

QUESTIONS

- *Think of an entrepreneur whom you admire. Check this list of attributes against those found in that person. How many does he or she have?*

- *Do these attributes describe you?*

- *Which attributes are your strengths? Which are your weaknesses?*

ACTION

- *List those attributes that you believe describe yourself. Get feedback from three people who know you well to determine whether others see you the same way.*

THE PROPER SOIL

—∽∞∽—

VISION AND PASSION

Although the proper climate is necessary to suc-cessfully cultivate fine grapes, it won't matter unless you also choose the right soil. Because classic wine grapes (known as *Vitis vinifera*) are deep-rooted plants, the soil cannot have impervious clay substratum or toxic concentrations of salt. The largest vines and heaviest crops are produced on deep, fertile soil. On our property, we have 36 feet of topsoil and we produce ten tons of grapes per acre.

Vision is the soil fertility for your business venture. The depth and breadth of your vision will determine how your business grows. It is not enough to have a well-defined vision. You must also articulate that vision and get others to see it, or the growth of your venture will stagnate.

When I started Captura Software, I had a vision for the future of expense management. Only two percent of all companies in the United States had automated the process of reporting travel and entertainment ex-penses. I had seen hundreds of people over the years sitting on airplanes with piles of receipts, filling out a spreadsheet-like report in order to get reimbursed for their expenses. I had also attended dozens of income tax audits when I ran a tax practice in Seattle, where I would watch an IRS agent spend hours reconciling paper receipts to the amounts recorded on a tax return.

I envisioned an entirely new way of handling expenses, where an employee could use a credit card for all T&E expenses and then retrieve those charges with the click of a mouse. Without sorting any receipts, an individual would then merely add any out-of-pocket expenses and, with another click of a button, submit all expenses to corporate headquarters. With the policy of the company neatly translated into automated rules (per Gerald's idea), these expenses could be checked against policy and then passed on immediately to the accounting department for reimbursement. The employee could receive a direct deposit to his or her checking account within hours of returning home.

It was the clarity of this vision in my mind that helped me inspire others to join Captura to develop the product and later helped me convince venture capitalists to invest their money in the company.

The key to having others share your vision (which is absolutely necessary for your long-term success) is to be *very* clear about it yourself. I could see my product in use many years before it became a reality. I could see the kind of company Captura would be (the hundreds of employees, the worldwide offices, the press coverage) even when there were only eight of us sharing an uncarpeted office space where we could see into the offices below through the holes in the floor. I dreamed a dream and then made it come true. You must be able to do the same.

When my husband and I found the property where our vineyard currently sits, it was covered with weeds and redwood trees and looked better suited for sandlot ball. That was what I saw, but within an hour of walking the property with Christopher, I could see rows and rows of vines stretching to the horizon. It was easy to see them once Christopher described his vision to me. It took him two years to remove more than 200 trees, turn the soil, lay out the vineyard, install the trellis, and plant the vines. As I write, I am looking out over acres of vines that appear exactly as he described them to me more than four years ago. He held onto his vision every step of the way.

You must have a vision.

Although fertile soil is a must for producing bountiful crops, soil structure is even more critical when growing wine grapes. If the soil contains any obstruction to root penetration, it will not matter how fertile your soil is, because root development will be impaired. Our 36 feet of topsoil is "stratum-free," meaning there are no layers of clay or other impervious soil to stop the roots from fully exploring the soil. That is one reason Christopher is able to get such a high yield of grapes.

The "soil structure" that you will need as an entrepreneur is passion. This is the "stratum-free soil" that will bring your vision to life and allow it to be fully explored.

Most people find it easy to have a dream or a vision for themselves. Talk to people who have played the lottery and ask them what they would do with the money if they won. They will tell you exactly how they plan to spend their winnings, down to the details of the house they will buy, the car they will drive, and even the clothes they will wear. They have already envisioned it. Vision alone is not enough, however. It's like a car without gas. Your vision will not become real without energy to fuel it toward action. That is where passion comes in.

Over and over, I have heard this word applied to me. People will tell me that they love my passion or that they cannot believe how passionate I am or that they wish they had as much passion about their life as I have about mine. I have also heard this word applied to my husband. After spending ten minutes with him in his small winery, they will often remark, "Chris sure is passionate about wine, isn't he?"

This is usually said by people who are trying to move on with their day and have gotten "trapped" with him discussing wine. He will immerse you in conversation about malectic fermentation or the 1994 Bernard Pradel Cabernet, and you will not be seen again for hours.

The funny thing about passion is that it is a fuel that can ignite a fire in yourself and in others. My good friend Jim is a great example of this concept. Jim has a passion for restoring old automobiles. At any given time, he will have two or three restorations underway in his barn, from 1932 Ford trucks to 1948 woody station wagons. I don't know anything about classic cars, but after ten minutes listening to Jim critique the woodwork, the grillwork, or even the paint job, I have "caught the bug" and suddenly find myself wanting to join him in working on one of the cars. In order to break the spell, I have to remind myself how much I abhor tedious work.

That's how passion works. You catch it.

I have spent a lot of time thinking about this thing called "passion." I wonder why some people have it and some don't, where it comes from, and what you can do to get it. Have you ever noticed that people with passion tend to be passionate about more than one thing? I think that is because passion is a deeply ingrained part of one's psyche rather than a simple emotion. I love to read biographies. I think if someone has led a life worthy of a biography, he or she possesses this characteristic of "passion."

I have yet to meet an entrepreneur who was passionless. The most successful entrepreneurs possess a passion that is contagious and limitless. Walt Disney was passionate about entertainment. First it was cartoons, then movies, and then a theme park. When he saw *The Jazz Singer* in 1927, he became convinced that his beloved Mickey Mouse would have to be seen as well as heard. He envisioned *Steamboat Willie* long before he made it, and he used his passion and excitement to convince others to invest more than $15,000 to produce it. It was an elaborate undertaking with more than 20,000 hand-crafted frames and a fully orchestrated soundtrack. When it premiered, it was an overnight sensation. It was not just the phenomenon of a talking Mickey that made the film a success; it was the hours and hours of energy expended in turning the vision into reality. Walt Disney had passion.

You cannot fake passion. You cannot acquire passion. You cannot manufacture passion. But I believe we all possess it. Passion resides in that place within all of us that we have defined as our "heart." You just need to access it.

Benjamin Disraeli said, "Man is only truly great when he acts from his passion." Without passion, we are merely latent possibility. The key is to recognize where your passion lies and unleash it toward your vision.

QUESTIONS

- *What have you been most passionate about in your life?*

- *How did you act and what did you accomplish when you felt that passionate?*

- *How does that passion relate to your business endeavor? If it doesn't, how can it?*

Actions

- *Describe your vision for your business in writing. When you read it, do you feel excited? If someone else were to read it, would he or she experience your passion? Why or why not?*

- *Record in a journal those times in your life when you were truly passionate about a job, a cause, or a person. What do you notice about yourself when you are passionate?*

MATCHING CLIMATE WITH SOIL

—∿∿—

THE PERSONAL MISSION STATEMENT

Even the most passionate person will sometimes lose touch with his passion. Unfortunately, this often happens when it is needed the most (such as when meeting with a banker for a loan when payroll is due). A tool that I have found helpful in accessing my passion and channeling it toward my vision, no matter how weary I am, is the personal mission statement.

I learned of the importance of mission statements from Stephen Covey's fabulous book *The Seven Habits of Highly Effective People*. In his apt words, a personal mission statement "focuses on what you want to be (character) and to do (contributions) and on the values and principles upon which being and doing are based. It is fundamentally changeless."

Your mission statement can be as brief or as lengthy as you want. For me, a short mission statement works better. It is my personal anchor. It reminds me why I am here. It keeps me focused on my purpose and helps me get in touch with my passion.

My personal mission statement is "to promote,

model, and influence the fulfillment of individual potential for all those around me." This simple statement sums up what I want to do as a mother, a wife, an entrepreneur, an author, a teacher, and a community member. It does not define what I do for a living or how I do it, but it gives my life meaning each and every day. I started my career teaching second grade and now I am a CEO. My job has changed, but my mission is the same. I am passionate about growth — both my own and other people's. By connecting with my mission, I can tap into my passion when I need to encourage my children to do their homework, to motivate my employees, to get out of bed at 5:00 a.m. to go to my work-out. I connect with my purpose — fulfilling potential — and the energy comes.

Writing a personal mission statement is not a trivial task. Many fine books are available that can assist you in crafting yours. The important thing is to create it so that it reflects your uniqueness and gives you a sense of purpose. It is a powerful way to harness your passion toward your vision and to keep you focused on that which is important to you in your life. And anyone who is building a business will have lots of opportunities to need reminding of what is important in life.

QUESTIONS

- *What is at the center of your life?*

- *What contribution would you most want to be remembered for?*

- *What do you feel makes you unique?*

ACTION

- *Write a personal mission statement that describes your purpose and provides meaning and motivation for you.*

Structure of the Vine

THE WINEGROWER USUALLY thinks of the vine as the unit in grape production. Each vine is capable of carrying out all the processes necessary to its life and its perpetuation. To carry on these processes, the vine has developed separate parts, each with a special function. These parts may be classified into two groups by the work they perform: those that carry on vegetative activity and those that produce seeds or fruit. The roots, trunk, shoots, and leaves are primarily concerned with keeping the vine alive, through functions such as absorbing water and minerals from the soil, manufacturing carbohydrates and other foods in the leaves, and respiration. These parts are commonly referred to as the rootstock.

The flowers, on the other hand, produce seeds and fruit — in the wild, preserving the life of the species and, under cultivation, supplying man with grapes, raisins, and wine.

The entrepreneur usually thinks he or she is the only unit necessary for a business to grow. However, a vineyard is never built with just one vine.

Your vision is what gives life to the business in the

beginning. Then it will be your day-to-day work that will keep the business going. But to truly grow your business, you will need to select the proper team to help you. I do not believe any single individual possesses all the skills necessary to build a business. Without other "vines" to plant in your soil, you will have a pitiful crop. But as any grower will tell you, you must select the right vines.

Selecting Rootstock

—⟋⟍—

The Need for Team

There are hundreds of types of rootstock available worldwide. The best results are achieved when the rootstock and the soil type are perfectly matched.

In Sonoma County, around ten common rootstocks are utilized according to the rootstock vigor preferred. Since Sonoma and Napa have experienced a major infestation of *Phylloxera* (a root louse that destroys vines), it is important for a grower in this area to select rootstock that is resistant to this particular pest. In addition, rootstock is matched with the plans for irrigation. If a vineyard is "dry-farmed," the rootstock will need very deep roots. On the other hand, if the vineyard has drip irrigation, the rootstock can have much shallower roots.

The soil on our property is sandy loam (officially known as "Yolo loam"). One important factor in selecting rootstock for our soil was the depth of the roots. Because Christopher wanted to control the water and nutrients that the vines would get, he had to search for a rootstock that would send roots down five to ten feet, where drip irrigation can be used to control the rate of water and nutrients the roots receive.

After much reading and consultation with Sonoma Grapevines, a nursery specializing in grapevines, Christopher selected a rootstock called Couderc 3309 (*Vitis riparia x Vitis rupestris*) because it produces vines of low to moderate vigor in deep fertile loams and has a good resistance to *Phylloxera*. It has been a resounding success for our soil and our climate.

In building a team for Captura, I knew I would have to find people who would be willing to do any job and could afford to take the risk of receiving little or no pay (they needed deep roots because we did not have much water!). Fortunately, the perfect people were all to be found among the folks with whom I had worked previously. Because they had at one time worked for a start-up software company, they knew what they were in for; because it had been a successful company that went public, several of them were able financially to take on the risk. Unfortunately, the perfect place to plant the Captura "vineyard" happened to be in Seattle.

I often am asked, "Why Seattle?" It seems to make little sense that I would locate a company two states away from my home. The answer is really very simple. Seattle was where the best "rootstock" was located, in the form of *Vitis Corey, Vitis Joe,* and *Vitis Jeffrey.*

These are the three men who make up the core development team at Captura. Having an idea is one thing, and turning that idea into a company is another thing, but making the product is the biggest thing. The problem we were trying to solve involved very complex technical concepts, not the least of which was how to handle the data integrity between the corporate computer system and the travelers who would be submitting expense reports from remote computers. Corey, Joe, and Jeffrey had been working together for years and had most recently created a sales force automation package that utilized the latest in emerging technology to address many of the issues we were facing with our Employee Payables product concept.

One of the most wonderful things about software is

that it is a creative and collaborative effort where you build something out of nothing. Corey is my friend, my co-founder, my CTO, and an all-around wonderful guy. He is one of the most talented software developers I have ever known. He has both vision and passion about technology, and he built a great team by bringing Joe and Jeffrey into his previous company to counterbalance his skills. Together, they agreed to join Captura to build our product. Because such talent is so rare, I decided to locate the company on their home turf. (Of course, the presence right down the road of the world's largest software company helped draw some of the best and brightest, thus improving the quality of the local talent pool.) And, because I had spent most of my adult life in Seattle, it was already a place I knew and loved.

My other co-founders were still in southern California, where we had all worked together. When you plant a vineyard, the ideal is to have all the land in one contiguous parcel in order to have maximum control of the crop. Although we tried the "virtual company" approach for awhile, we found that the same principle holds true for software companies, so three of the other co-founders relocated their families to Washington state in order to be part of Captura.

One of them, Jennifer, was a brilliant young woman

whom I had hired years earlier and who was happily settled in a new home and content with her job. When I met with her for lunch to explain the opportunity, she was definitely not interested in moving to Seattle. She was a native Californian with her entire family close by and believed the bad press about all the rain in the Pacific Northwest. I kept using my passion to persuade her. Finally, she relented, and both she and her husband (who also had worked for me previously) sold their house, packed up, and moved to Washington because of the power of passion. Months later, when we could not make payroll and it appeared we would have to shut the doors, I couldn't help but think about the wise words of Max DePree, who says that leadership "is a serious meddling in other people's lives."

After you plant the vine, you then must tend it. The successful grower never forgets that. In fact, in France, growers call the vines their "children." As an entrepreneur, you need other people to help you make your dream come true, but once they have committed to following your course with you, you must not neglect them. Now, I visit my young protégée and her husband out on their five-acre parcel with their dream house, and we laugh about how we'll tell their kids the story of how they came to be Washingtonians!

QUESTIONS

- *What are the most important qualities that you need in your team?*

- *Which members of your team exemplify the type of person you need for your rootstock? Why?*

- *How are you nurturing your newly planted rootstock?*

ACTION

- *Identify the attributes that someone must have to be successful in your business environment.*

The Root System

—⚬∾—

The Right People

The primary functions of roots are absorption of water and mineral nutrients, storage of reserves, and anchorage. Once a vine is planted in the vineyard, the roots hold it permanently in place. By the time the desired form of the vine is obtained, five to eight years after planting, vines are largely self-supporting. The roots have become strong enough to hold the stem upright, and the stem is rigid enough not to bend under the weight of the shoots, leaves, and fruit.

When selecting the core team members for your business, you must remember that they will become the root system for your vines. They will be called upon to fulfill many important functions.

After the pain of selecting and de-selecting team members, I have concluded that the best people for a start-up possess three qualities important above all others. I refer to these people as "TIPsters"; they have Tenacity, Integrity, and Passion in unusual abundance. They are those unique individuals who do what they say they will, have fun doing it, and never give up. They are the key to your success. A lot of searching may be needed to find them, but once found, they will make all the difference in the quality of the crop and your ability to withstand all kinds of pests and droughts.

One of Captura's founders, Bill, really demonstrated the qualities of a TIPster. We had worked together at another company, but didn't know each other well. He had worked in sales, and I had been in development and support. In Captura's early days, he was at first uncertain how to contribute, since we did not have anything to sell yet. Instead of doing the job he was most skilled at (selling), he took whatever task came along and was tenacious about getting it done. When we finally did have a product to sell, he was extraordinarily creative about figuring out ways to travel on a shoestring in order to make sales calls, because we had no travel budget. He never gave up, even in the most trying circumstances. He is as committed an individual as I have ever known.

Once you have a team of this kind of people, you will be amazed at how you can overcome any obstacle.

After the initial year of product development at Captura, we had run out of money. With no customers in sight and no venture capitalists willing to back a company seeking to break into an unproven market, I was in a bit of turmoil about what to do to keep the business alive. Rather than try to figure it out by myself, I brought my team members together and asked for their advice. They came up with a plan whereby we would have a contest to find the first customer (with 100 shares of Captura stock for the winner). Although mostly software engineers (Bill being the main exception), they felt that if we all simply tapped our networks we would surely find one company willing to be a "beta" customer. They took on this challenge with a tenacity that was inspirational. An entire firm of development folks turned into salespeople overnight. In the end, there was a tie between two teams, each of which landed a customer at the same time.

This episode was a turning point in the company's history, and it happened because we had tenacious, committed people.

QUESTIONS

- *Do your employees share a passionate commitment to the business? Why or why not?*

- *What rewards do people get for taking the risk with you?*

ACTION

- *Create a plan to reward your "TIPsters" for their commitment.*

VINEYARD MANAGEMENT

—ന്ന—

A COACH

Even though a vineyard owner wants to make all decisions himself and aspires to control all aspects of his vineyard, the wise farmer knows the importance of getting guidance from others. In Sonoma County, we have several vineyard management firms. These companies provide services ranging from fully managing your vineyard property to providing specific maintenance activities, such as spraying or pruning. They have hundreds of acres under management and therefore have a wealth of information for the small vineyard owner to draw upon.

Although Christopher had some experience and schooling in viticulture, he believed that the smartest way to assure the success of his vineyard was to hire the services of a vineyard management firm to work with him as he planted and developed his business.

Likewise, although I had some experience and background in software, I felt that my best chances for success depended on finding a guide. Enter Barbara — coach, mentor, and friend. Just as Christopher would not have a successful vineyard today without the assistance of a vineyard management company, Captura would not exist if not for Barbara's guidance and involvement.

Stories about Barbara could fill a book. Her high energy is impossible to ignore and has a positive effect on everyone she meets. Barbara is an extremely passionate woman committed to making a difference in people's lives. She definitely made a difference for me.

Barbara went into consulting after twenty years in the telecommunications industry because she decided she wanted to work with young companies and assist them in their individual and team development. She is particularly skilled at teaching people how to communicate effectively, which is as important to a business as sun is to a vineyard. I first met her at my former company when one of my employees brought her in to help us manage the tremendous growth we experienced after the company went public.

Once I had my Captura team in place, I hired her to coach me in my new role as CEO and to facilitate the creation of our mission and corporate culture. Although passion and vision are necessary ingredients for every entrepreneur, they are also the qualities that can get us into trouble. Without an objective eye to tell you the truth, you may find yourself off planting vines in fields with sandy soil and no water.

Barbara has been at my side to challenge and encourage me through each new step. With her wisdom, insight, and guidance, I was able to plant and grow my Captura vineyard with confidence. She taught me the importance of coaching as a management model, and many of the ideas and thoughts presented in this book originated with her. She is the vineyard worker who has walked many a mile in many a vineyard and has seen it all. Every entrepreneur needs to have someone to provide another perspective and to contribute insights, experience, and just plain common sense (something visionaries tend to be a bit short on!). Charles Merrill had Edmund Lynch. Bill Gates had Paul Allen. Walt Disney had Roy. I had Barbara.

QUESTIONS

- *Do you have a coach or mentor?*

- *How effectively are you using your coach?*

- *If you do not have a coach, where can you find one?*

ACTION

- *Create a plan and a budget to make outside counsel part of your plan for building your business.*

Establishing the Vineyard

ESSENTIAL TO ANY vineyard's success is a favorable combination of locale, variety of grapes, and proper utilization of the crop. Locality and variety are self-explanatory. Utilization refers to how a particular variety of grape will be used in the winemaking process; for example, Syrah grapes should be used to make Syrah wine, and not blended with other grapes. The famous Riesling wines of Germany, the splendid Ohañez grapes of Spain, and the fabulous Zinfandel grapes of my own Dry Creek Valley cannot be easily duplicated in other parts of the world. They are supreme largely because they are uniquely suited to the regions where they are produced. A lot of patience and experimentation went into finding the right combination of variety and climate.

Essential to success in building your business is a favorable combination of market opportunity, resources, and timing. Finding that proper mix will take as much patience, experimentation, and luck as it did for those long-ago growers. If you review the stories of other fabled entrepreneurs, you will see this combination at work.

For example, as a milkshake machine salesman, Raymond Kroc routinely paid visits to clients. But when the 52-year-old salesman traveled from his home near Chicago to southern California to meet two of his biggest clients, the combination of timing, resources, and opportunity aligned, and the result was anything but routine. What he saw in San Bernardino was the drive-in restaurant of brothers Maurice and Richard McDonald.

"Something was definitely happening here, I told myself," Kroc later wrote in his autobiography *Grinding It Out.* "This had to be the most amazing merchandising operation I'd ever seen." Kroc felt sure the McDonalds' operation could succeed wildly if it expanded. So the next day, he persuaded them to cut a deal, thus revolutionizing the American restaurant industry.

In 1994, when we first conceived of the idea for Captura, it was impossible to automate the filing of T&E reports. The Internet was not yet widely available, few traveling employees had access to a computer, and the IRS still required paper receipts for almost every expense. So although I had the market opportunity (only two percent of all companies had automated this task) and the resources, my timing was off. When the World Wide Web took off in 1995 and the IRS issued a new ruling regarding electronic credit card receipts in 1996, the favorable conditions we had awaited were suddenly in place. But the wait was very painful and it could have been less so had I done a better job of determining the market's interest in our product.

CHOOSING A LOCATION

—m—

ANALYZING YOUR MARKET

When selecting a tract of land, even in prime winegrowing regions such as Sonoma or Napa, the grower must study the characteristics of the particular piece of property to determine the type of grapes that can be grown with the greatest likelihood of success. Identifying the grape that produces wine that consumers will like and that grows well and ripens consistently in the prevailing climate is perhaps the single most important decision a winemaker makes in the quest for high-quality wine. Likewise, identifying the proper market opportunity for a product is the single most important decision you will make as an entrepreneur.

When Christopher decided to re-enter the wine industry by planting a vineyard, he created the following criteria for himself. First, the grape had to be one that would produce wine that appealed to him; second, it had to be a grape that other wineries would buy. Since more Cabernet Sauvignon and Chardonnay are produced and purchased than any other variety, his decision would have been simple, if only those wines excited him. But, as he is fond of saying, he is a devoted member of the "ABC" Club — Anything But Cabernet (or Chardonnay). Therefore, he spent a lot of time researching the market, which involved tasting many wines (much more fun than the market research I have to do in my field), before deciding on Syrah. Also called "Shiraz" by the Australians, Syrah grapes produce a red rhone-style wine which has a peppery and full-bodied taste and goes well with spicy foods.

In 1994, when he first chose his grape, less than two percent of all vineyards in Sonoma were planted to Syrah, but his intuition (and his palate) told him this would be a wine for the future. Fortunately, our property is very well suited to growing Syrah. Now, in 1998, acres of other varietals (such as French Colombard) are being pulled out to make room for new vineyards of Syrah.

Before you start any kind of business, you must have an in-depth understanding of the industry you are entering and the customers you will be serving. You should join the trade association for your type of business. The association and its members will have a wealth of information which they have gained through experience. You should gather information about trends affecting your industry's products, services, expenses, rate of growth, and technological changes. You should know whether you are entering an industry that is experiencing growth or one that is mature. By understanding the nature of your industry, you will be better able to identify the specific market you should enter.

It is on this point that I made what was nearly a fatal flaw in building my own business. After spending fifteen years in the accounting industry (with a decade of that specifically in the accounting software industry), I thought I knew both my industry (software) and my customers (chief financial officers) very well. I had *no* marketing or sales background and I didn't understand the importance of analyzing the market. If I had, I would have found out that enterprise software vendors spend an average of $15 million and three years bringing a product to the market. That sure would have been helpful information to factor into my six-month, $250,000 business plan.

I also would have discovered many interesting

reasons *why* only two percent of the companies had automated their T&E expenses. If I had surveyed my potential customers, I would have understood that they did not perceive any benefit from the automation of expense reporting. But I did not do any research or analysis. I subscribed to the school of marketing thought that said, "Build it and they will come."

Well, we built it and — they didn't come.

In 1995, companies were not ready to spend thousands of dollars to automate a process that seemed to be working just fine. Even though the manual process of filing expense reports was time-consuming for employees and tedious for accounting staff, it was not inconvenient enough to prompt companies to seek a different solution. Corporate America did not see the need for my product, and I had no marketing background to understand concepts such as "creating a demand" or "missionary selling."

So, I went back to the drawing board with Corey, Joe, and Jeffrey. We came up with an even "cooler" way to build it, and customers still didn't come.

Meanwhile, while we were building the most elaborate product with the coolest technology, the people who did come calling were the landlord, the IRS, and the bill collectors. They didn't care how cool my product was; they wanted to get paid. And even though the customers did eventually come, I put good people through unnecessary pain because I did not do my job adequately. I cannot emphasize enough the importance of market research.

The great thing about the World Wide Web (gotta love technology!) is that tons of market information is available to you literally at your fingertips. Want to know how many companies are out there selling your same product? Use a search engine and find out. Want to know exactly what your competition is up to? Go to their web sites. Want to read every article published about your market? Just look it up! It couldn't be easier.

QUESTIONS

- *What are the significant trends in your industry?*

- *What is the total size of your target market? What data is that based on?*

- *How much money is spent on purchasing the type of goods or services you offer?*

- *Have you segmented your market? Which segments have you targeted?*

- *How many businesses are already in the mar-ketplace? Do you know their strengths and weaknesses?*

- *Do you have a detailed customer profile?*

ACTION

- *Write a marketing strategy framework that addresses the following topics:*

  The Promise: *What is the promise associated with your products or services?*

  The Problem: *What problem is the customer experiencing currently?*

  The Solution: *How will your product or service address the problem?*

  Compelling Value Proposition: *How is your solution unique and different from other solutions?*

  Target Audience: *Who will you sell this solution to? Be specific.*

  Adoption Cycle: *Where is the market in adopt-ing solutions like this?*

Market Segmentation: *How will you segment the market?*

Competitive Analysis: *Who are your main competitors? What are their strengths and weaknesses?*

Strategic Alliances: *What industry alliances or partnerships will be necessary to market your product or service?*

Positioning and Messaging Direction: *What will your key messages be? How will you position yourself against the competition?*

Planning the Vineyard

—꣸—

The Organizational Structure

In vineyards where power implements are used, which is most modern vineyards, economical handling demands careful planning. Long, evenly spaced rows, with adequate turning space at the ends, make cultivation easier. Widely spaced vines are cheaper to cultivate than closely planted vines, because larger and more efficient implements can be used. Vine spacing is one of many considerations in planning a vineyard and varies widely among the different grape-growing regions of the world. In the Champagne region of France, vines are planted 3,000 or more to the acre, to ensure full yields in this cool region. In our vineyard, there are only several hundred vines per acre, owing to the hot climate and vigorous nature of our soil.

Whether you envision a sole proprietorship or a large corporation, you should take great care to arrange the proper legal, financial, and organizational structure.

To this end, you must devise a business plan, a document that outlines in detail this framework and a timetable for putting it in place. Your business plan will help you clearly define whether or not you have enough room for all the "vines" you will be planting. The probability of success in a new business endeavor is directly related to the extent that your business plan is accurate and complete. Once you have completed your "Strategic Marketing Framework," a big part of the business plan is already complete.

I did not write my business plan until I needed to raise money from outside investors. That was a *big* mistake. A business plan is your blueprint for building a successful business and is the single most important tool for avoiding costly mistakes.

There are many good books and software programs that can guide you through the creation of a business plan. You will want to be sure you address the following topics:

- The market opportunity
- The financial objectives and growth
- The legal form of organization and ownership
- A profile of the management team and an organizational chart
- A basis for financing the business
- A timetable for establishing the business

I have already shared with you some of the problems Captura faced because I did not define the market opportunity or the financial objectives. Now, I would like to address the problems I faced due to the lack of a formal capital agreement and a clear organizational structure. When we started Captura (or "Newco" as we referred to it for months before settling on a name), we simply threw some money in a bank account and started designing a product. Six of us were involved in the very beginning and, other than a vague idea of roles based upon our previous jobs, we didn't take the time to create job descriptions or discuss responsibilities. To give you an idea of how we were operating, here are the titles we established at our first meeting:

- "Mr. Looking Good" (for Bill, our chief sales guy)
- "CoreMan" (for Corey, our system architect)
- "Boy" (for Jeffrey, the youngest)
- "Code Policeman" (for Joe, the one in charge of the standards)
- "Alex P. Keaton" (for John, our main financial guy)
- "BullDog" (for me, the "get-it-done" person)

Get the picture? We were having lots of fun, had built lots of trust over the years, and didn't see the need for a hierarchy (except for Joe, whom I would like to acknowledge officially for trying to get us all to see the error of our way even then). We also had no legal or formal written agreements relating to employment, stock price, sweat equity, stock options, or ownership. I am embarrassed to admit that the situation remained that way for almost twelve months. I am not sure whether to be flattered by the level of trust among the team members or appalled by my lack of responsibility to the team.

Only when the newness of the adventure had worn off, the bank account had dwindled, and we realized we would have to go outside of our tight-knit group to raise additional capital did I get serious. I wrote a business plan, established a capital structure, and forced the adoption of formal roles and responsibilities within the team. Suffice it to say, an upheaval ensued that almost led to the dissolution of the firm. Since we all had assumptions about our individual stakes in the company and everyone's role, we ended up with expectations not being met, which diminished the trust among us. Some members of the team had invested large sums of cash and worked without pay that first year. Some had drawn minimal salaries. Others had invested cash, but only worked part-time. You can guess what happened. Everyone thought they were entitled to a large percentage of ownership in exchange for their cash, labor, or talent; without clear, upfront agreements, how could I reconcile it fairly? At the end of the day, there is only 100 percent of a company to give out and the "cash is king" reality had to prevail. We made it through that difficult time, but not without damaging relationships that took a long time to mend.

The moral of this story is that you need to make all the decisions regarding the ownership of your company before you recruit anyone *and* you must clearly communicate, in writing, the terms to each person. Get the best legal and professional counsel you can afford and follow their advice. Being an entrepreneur means assuming the risk; it does not mean you know everything about business.

Questions

- *Have you clearly defined the capital structure of your business?*

- *Have you projected the initial capital requirements, the cash flow for the first year, the key operating ratios, and the projected sources of debt and equity financing?*

- *Do you have an attorney and an accountant well versed in your type of business?*

Actions

- *If you have not already done so, hire an accountant and an attorney specializing in your industry.*

- *Write your complete business plan and submit it to outside business advisors for feedback.*

- *Write job descriptions for all the key positions within the company. Include specific levels of authority and responsibility.*

THE TRELLIS SYSTEM

—ɯɯ—

THE COMPANY MISSION STATEMENT

Grapevines cannot be grown satisfactorily without some form of support. Until the early 1920s, vineyards in California were still being developed without supports, but growers were realizing that the extra costs from labor, delayed bearing, and operating a vineyard of poorly formed vines were greater than the expense of constructing suitable stakes and trellises. In building a business, your company mission and guiding principles will act as the support for your vision. If you take the time to craft a mission, you will achieve the same results as the grower who invests in a trellis system — a uniformity in corporate culture that sustains growth.

I have found that, in business, this kind of activity is considered "nice to do" but often is not viewed as a core business activity. It has been my experience that a mission is as central to a successful business as a budget or a business plan. Without an aligned vision and shared values, a company cannot survive.

I also know that people cannot talk about values and principles without emotions. That is what makes such discussion difficult in today's business environment. We have become so concerned with being "professional" that we believe it is inappropriate to bring our personal beliefs and philosophies into the workplace. I am forever grateful to Stephen Covey for reintroducing the concept of missions and principles back into the business world. I am encouraged that the success of his books *The Seven Habits of Highly Effective People* and *Principle-Centered Leadership* (both required reading at Captura) means that most people are eager to bring more of themselves into their professional environments.

Because this topic makes people uncomfortable, I have found that the only way to address it is to take everyone away from the day-to-day office environment. That way, you can create an environment where people feel safe to share the important ideas, thoughts, and feelings that are the true genesis for building teams and missions.

Many stories are told at Captura of the various off-site meetings held throughout the years. Some have become so apocryphal that they are part and parcel of the company's cultural identity.

I have found each and every off-site meeting incredibly valuable to my personal growth and the growth of the organization. We continue to hold them regularly, and now employees strive to design ever more creative "out-of-the-box" experiences.

We have held off-sites at the vineyard where attendees harvested grapes and made an abundant meal from foodstuffs they found growing on the property. We have written and shared personal mission statements, composed songs, gone on scavenger hunts, and even washed feet!

Just last week, through my office window, I saw the finance and operations staff in the parking lot walking together atop two beams that were connected with ropes. The office manager was shouting out the cadence and there was my CFO, hanging on to his controller for dear life when he missed the count.

I have learned from Barbara that people learn best from experience. It is one thing to talk about trust and quite another to fall off a picnic table backwards and trust your team to catch you. All our Captura off-site meetings are adventures, but none was as important as the very first where we established our "trellis."

One of my first acts as CEO was to bring everyone together in Healdsburg in March of 1995 for two days. After a few months of referring to our endeavor as the "Newco" company, we had finally agreed on calling our new enterprise "Captiva" because we were going to "capture" data (later changed to Captura because IBM already had ownership of the Captiva name). I felt the time had arrived to create our mission statement.

After completing some pre-meeting assignments (Meyers-Briggs tests, goal-setting, etc.), the team members came from points south and north and convened at the San Francisco airport. From there, they were given an assignment to have lunch at the LoLo Café in Santa Rosa, take a picture in front of the restaurant, and arrive in Healdsburg by noon. Without directions, they had to exercise innovation to find the restaurant and then, when it was closed, to find another way to fulfill the assignment, which they creatively did by buying fast food and eating it on the curb in front of the café.

They arrived on time, not without some anxiety about what in the heck we were going to do for two days in the wine country. We had hired Alan, our first employee outside the founders' group, just the week before. I am sure that on the first day of the off-site he thought he had joined a really bizarre company, because we went on wine scavenger hunts and wrote personal mission statements starting with "I am. . . ."

After team-building experiences involving outdoor activities, we settled down to the work of combining all our personal mission statements into a corporate mission statement. That process took a full day as it was done with the serious intent to assure that our mission statement would reflect not only individual contributions but also would be as relevant years from now as it was the day it was written. Although lengthy, it has held up incredibly well and has been used time and time again to keep us on track as we faced new decisions. I keep the original handwritten flipchart version in my office as a reminder of this important work.

The mission created on March 22, 1995, by the Captura founders is:

"Our mission is to create and sustain high-value customer relationships by delivering highly usable, workflow-based business solutions in a challenging, respectful, and team-oriented environment that promotes dedication, pursuit of excellence, innovation, and creativity so that Captura Software, Inc., will ascend to market dominance and realize an enviable financial position."

Even though we knew we were building a specific expense-management application in 1995, we wanted the company focus to be on the "workflow-based business solutions" and on "high-value customer relationships." Every time we have faced decisions about the product or the distribution or the technology, we have gone back to review our mission. By having a mission and following it, we have made the right choices which have led to our success.

When Merrill Lynch completed its pilot test of our product and was ready to start the roll-out to its 50,000 employees, the event was marked with an evening sailboat ride around Manhattan. Two key Capturians, John and Phil, were invited — they had literally lived in hotels and spent 24-hour shifts at Merrill Lynch to assure the product was performing. At the dinner, a Merrill Lynch vice president handed out T-shirts that said, "Merrill Lynch is Bullish on Captura Software" and gave John and Phil personal gifts demonstrating how well Merrill Lynch's executives knew them (Jolt Colas, Rollos, and box of McDonald-type playballs for John's son). I can't think of a better example of "creating and sustaining a high-value customer relationship."

QUESTIONS

- *Do you have a company mission statement?*

- *Did your team participate in writing the mission statement?*

- *What can you do to facilitate the creation of a meaningful mission statement?*

ACTION

- *Create a mission statement using the following suggestions, which are reprinted here with the permission of Fagan and Associates:*

  1. *Always structure mission statements from the bottom up. Start with individuals, then move up to departments, then to divisions, and then to the company.*

  2. *Involve everyone in the process so there is shared ownership of the mission.*

  3. *Use a waterfall model like this:*
     Our mission is to . . .
     In a way that . . .
     So that . . .

  4. *Do not rush the process. The creation of a good mission statement requires time.*

NOTES

THE
POWER
OF
PRINCIPLES

It is often easier to fight
for principles than
to live up to them.
— Adlai Stevenson

THE CYCLE OF THE VINE

LIKE ALL OF NATURE, the vine follows a predictable annual cycle. In the spring, tiny buds appear which soon send out their shoots along with the leaves and clusters. After a period of rapid growth, during which shoots can lengthen as much as an inch a day, the flowers bloom, and the berries set. In the late summer, the berries ripen and, on the cue of the winemaker, the harvest occurs.

As a deciduous plant, the vine sheds its leaves in the fall in a beautiful show of color. Then through the winter, it rests dormant.

The next spring, the cycle begins again.

Many vineyards in the Dry Creek Valley are more than a century old and, although farming techniques have changed, they still bear their fruit each year in the same way they have done for the past ten decades. The grower and the winemaker can make any number of decisions that will influence the quality and quantity of the grapes, but they cannot really affect the growth process. Rain and frost can and do interrupt the best of human plans.

The growth of a vine is a simple and elegant process

bound by nature's fundamental laws. One reason I wanted to raise my children in an agricultural environment was to expose them to the natural rhythms of life. There is something humbling about being beholden to the earth for your bounty. You always know, in a tangible way, that you are not in control of the plan. This knowledge helps keeps other aspects of life in perspective and has taught me to identify fundamental truths that I apply throughout my life. Stephen Covey asserts a fundamental idea about principles, that they "are natural laws in the human dimension that are just as real, just as unchanging and unarguably 'there' as laws such as gravity are in the physical dimension." I believe this to be true; therefore, I have built my business on beliefs, philosophies, and principles.

TRAINING YOUNG VINES

—∽—

BRINGING ON NEW EMPLOYEES

In establishing a vineyard, the purpose of "training" is to produce vines capable of bearing a good quantity of high-quality fruit. While training and pruning the young vines, the grower must know the form desired in the mature vine. Otherwise, he will make mistakes and the mature vine will be defective. In some instances, poorly formed vines can be corrected, but correction is costly and always necessitates large wounds.

It takes most of the first two years after planting a vineyard to get the root system established well enough that a single strong cane can be developed into a trunk. To do this, the vine requires not only favorable conditions for growth, but also support and training during the spring and early summer. This involves staking the vines, removing all except the bud best placed for tying to the support, and the actual tying itself. Every time the vine grows eight to twelve inches, it is tied to the stake again. Three or more tyings are usually necessary during the all-important second year.

I barely saw Christopher during our vineyard's second year because he was out tying almost constantly. Because I was also out "tying" my Captura "vines," it was difficult for us to stop and compare notes. The problem with the training phase of building a business is that there is a limited timeframe for doing the work. And, as with the vines, if you make a mistake, it is costly to go back and fix it once the company has matured.

There came a day when we needed to expand Captura beyond the first wave of employees. Because our tight-knit group had created the mission statement, established the core values of our Captura "root system," and struggled through some hard times, we were like a family. Therefore, we needed to be very careful in "grafting" on to our original rootstock.

At Captura, the first new employees we hired were carefully selected and carefully nurtured. The first one, Matt, was new to the software industry. With a keen sense of humor and an equally keen mind, he fit into the Captura team with ease. Matt was so committed to the team that, even though he had a family to support, he was one of the first employees to offer to defer some of his salary when times got tough. His actions during those months showed me that our new grafted vines could be as strong as our old vines.

The second new hire during this time was Jason, who created the moniker "Capturian." Jason joined us first as a contractor and then decided to become a full-fledged member of the team. He did so even though he knew we were financially unstable, a factor of some importance to a young father such as himself. His brilliance in developing systems has saved our company both time and money, and he constantly demonstrates our principle of "treating each other as customers." With the proper training and tying, his vine has grown to greater height than many of the other vines in the Captura vineyard.

The third member who was part of the first expansion team was Maurice (better known as "Big Mo"). A creative and gifted programmer, Mo spent most of his first year with us tied to a cubicle and computer screen. But knowing that growth requires sunlight, we took Mo along to one of the biggest trade shows in our industry, where he could demonstrate the product in our booth. I will never forget how big his eyes were that first day as he surveyed the trade show floor or how proud he was when he realized that people knew of our company. With youthful exuberance, Mo came up to me, pointed to his Captura badge, and said, "Dana, people actually stop me because they want to know about our product. They actually know who we are. Can you believe it?"

Matt, Jason, and Mo were the beginning of the new varietals. Their grafts have held up over the years, and they are still thriving at Captura.

Not all your grafts will take and not all your vines will tie properly. When they do, though, the result will be vines that are stronger and heartier than they would have been otherwise.

Questions

- *How do you train and tie your staff?*

- *Who trained you and invested in your growth?*

- *What impact did that person have on your career path?*

Actions

- *Create an internal training program for your staff where you can introduce them to the mission and principles of the organization.*

- *Invest in career development courses for your employees.*

SUPPORT FOR YOUNG VINES

—∾∾—

GUIDING PRINCIPLES

One day a couple of years ago, upon returning home after my week in Seattle, I turned into our driveway and saw acres and acres of well-tilled soil studded with thousands of popsicle sticks. At first, I thought that my eight-year-old son David must have been playing and gotten bored. When I saw how neatly they were laid out, however, I realized this couldn't be the work of a child. In fact, each popsicle stick was painstakingly put in the ground to mark where individual stakes would be placed in order to support the vines.

While your mission is like the overall vineyard layout plan, your principles are the posts and stakes holding up the vines. Taking the time to carefully craft them will pay off over the years. You and your team members must create a set of guiding principles that your company can embrace and enforce and use to grow. Again, this work can only be accomplished by taking the time to carefully examine individual values and then jointly arrive at a set of principles you all share.

Below are the principles we formed at Captura

during our first month together. They are posted prominently in our offices, given to each new employee, and even featured on our web site. We challenge each other to follow them, and we continually strive to make decisions in alignment with our mission and our principles. One of my proudest moments at Captura came when I received my paycheck with a bright yellow notice attached to it stating the guiding principles of the Finance and Operations department. Staff members had developed their principles at an off-site meeting and wanted to share their "rules of conduct" with the entire company.

I truly believe that most people want to give meaning to their lives by following noble pursuits. When we tap into the deep, fundamental truths that we all share, we can reach heights together that we never could alone. That has been my experience at Captura as we have struggled through the bad times and celebrated the good times. Always, there was a well-established root system pointing the way to personal effectiveness and deep, rich relationships.

CAPTURA SOFTWARE GUIDING PRINCIPLES
We are a customer-oriented organization.
We create and sustain high-value relationships.

We expect commitment, accountability, and integrity from each other.

We care about quality of life and insist on personal/professional balance.

We are a learning organization and devote a portion of our budget and time to the professional development of our employees.

We value teamwork over individual contribution.

We are interested only in win/win solutions.

We focus on "what's possible" and are innovative in reaching decisions.

We seek to develop a diverse and multi-faceted team with a broad range of experience.

We do not make promises we cannot keep.

We value open and honest communication.

We are committed to quality in our product, our processes, and our relationships.

We are committed to growth — our own and other people's.

We are flexible and adaptable.

We are thoroughly committed to understanding our users and their needs.

We treat each other as customers.

QUESTIONS

- *As you read these guiding principles, are there any that you feel apply to your company? If so, which ones and why?*

- *What are the values that you want to build your principles around? Integrity? Loyalty? Service? Quality?*

ACTION

- *When building your guiding principles for the company, follow this model:*

  1. *Start by listing shared beliefs. A belief is something that is accepted as true.*
     For example: I believe that people are always in the process of growth.

  2. *Define the philosophy that supports the belief. Philosophy is the reasoning that supports a belief.*
     For example: My philosophy is that, because people are living beings, they must continuously grow as all living things do.

3. *Define the principle(s) inherent in your philosophy. A principle is a guideline or rule indicating how you will apply your belief and philosophy in your life.*

   For example: My principle is that I am committed to my own growth and to the growth of others.

TENDING YOUNG VINES

—⁓—

ACCOUNTABILITY IN LEADERSHIP

Once the vines are planted, staked, and tied, the grower's work really begins. Now comes the tending of the vines — daily walks through the vineyard looking for signs of pests or disease, constant vigilance and attention to weather, round-the-clock fertilizing and watering, and spraying and disking for weed control.

In the first two years of the development of our vineyard, Christopher never left the property. He was out in the vineyard every day and, during "grand growth," he was up two or three times a night putting fertilizer into the drip system. (After bearing three children, I have to confess that it was kind of nice to lie in bed while he "nursed" the baby.)

As an entrepreneur, not only are you called upon to be the catalyst and the visionary of your business endeavor, but you must also provide the leadership for your company. Your team will look to you for direction and guidance. You are the *one* person who must know where the company is going, why it is going there, and exactly how it will get there. If you cannot clearly and consistently communicate those three points, you are not tending your vineyard.

It is your clarity about your values and your behavior that sends messages about what is and is not important about the organization's operation. You provide the standard to which other people in the organization compare their own choices and behaviors. In order to set an example, you must know your principles.

A survey conducted by Human Resource Management examined the relationship between individual and organizational values. The research queried more than 2,300 managers from line supervisor to executive. The findings clearly reveal that the efforts of senior managers to clarify and articulate their personal values have a significant payoff for both leaders and their organizations. The studies show that shared values:

- Foster strong feelings of personal effectiveness.
- Promote high levels of company loyalty.
- Facilitate consensus about key organization goals.
- Encourage ethical behavior.
- Promote strong norms about working hard and caring.
- Reduce levels of job stress and tension.

In the fall of 1996, I faced a crisis at Captura. After

two years of development, we finally had a product ready to go. The only problem was that we had no money with which to market the product or even to pay the employees. I needed to foster company loyalty, facilitate consensus about our goals, and reduce the level of stress and tension.

At the same time that I was facing another month of telling my employees that they would once more need to take reduced pay, my husband was excitedly planning for his first harvest. Though he was still a year away from having the wine he so anticipated making, nonetheless he was celebrating this milestone in the realization of his vision. While everything was gloom and doom at Captura, the focus in the wine country was on the abundance of the season. We were personally broke, and I wasn't sure that either of our dreams would be realized, but I noticed that Christopher was still focused on his "end game" — the wine — while I was having trouble seeing past my current cash-flow crisis.

So, I made what appeared to my team to be a crazy decision. I used all my frequent flyer miles and what was left of my personal credit line to bring all my employees to the vineyard for two days to pick grapes. I wanted them to realize that we had created something of value and that, with our shared intentions and the right attitude, we would get through this difficult time. I wanted to share my personal values with my employees. I wanted to show them the value of hard work, diligence, passion, vision, and commitment. In addition to writing and sharing personal mission statements, each person also created a "treasure map," a collage representing those things in life that were most important to him or her. This is now a tradition with all new employees, and the collages are displayed throughout the office demonstrating the individual values that together make up our company.

I believe that those two days in Healdsburg formed a deep and lasting bond that got us through the next six months while we anxiously sought additional financing and revenue. The following August, after we had received a $2.5 million investment from Merrill Lynch, I took everyone out for dinner and a boat cruise on Lake Washington. At the center of each table was a bottle of "Captura" wine that had come out of the barrels only the week before. It helped to remind all of us of where we had been only nine months earlier and how much change we had undergone since then. Many of the employees still have and treasure their bottles as a symbol of what a difference shared vision and shared values can make.

I am reprinting here (with permission from the author) a letter I received following this off-site experience. The letter was from one of my fellow Capturians, Jim, who has been a tent pole of the organization. When I sprung the idea of this off-site on my management team, he was not at all convinced that we would gain any value from it, but he went along just the same. Here is the result of his experience, in his own words:

October 13, 1996

Dear Dana,

I am writing this to acknowledge, in a personal and permanent way, my profound respect for your leadership. It is difficult for me to express the impact this off-site has had on me.

I *wanted* to believe in the value of the off-site, but perhaps like St. Thomas, I had doubts. I needed to see to believe. Oh, I encouraged the team to be open to the experience, but with a tepid enthusiasm. I rationalized the potential value to them, impassionately. Now, as I write this, the irony is a little overwhelming.

The team's response to the challenge, the quality of their participation and the depth of their commitment was moving and powerful.

And because of this, it was probably *me* who was the most profoundly changed by the event.

I noted that you placed Healdsburg in the center of your Treasure Map. It only took two days of living there to understand why. Though, most significant to me is the fact that you've put this great treasure at risk to keep the Captura dream alive these past months. I am awed by such a genuine demonstration of commitment and the confidence you've displayed in the face of such uncertainty.

Like a thunderbolt it finally struck me that you draw your confidence *not* from the product, or the market or the technology, but from the people. It took this off-site for me to see that. And I really can see it because I now draw the same confidence from this inspiring group.

It may take more time for me to fully escape being your "Doubting Thomas," but I want you to always know that deep in my heart and with all my conviction, *I believe*. I believe in the team; I believe in the vision and I believe in you.

With all my respect and admiration,

Jim

As you can see, sharing your values with your team can be inspirational and motivational. This letter has hung on my wall for two years now, and continually reminds me of my responsibility as a leader.

QUESTIONS

- *What values do you want to share with your team?*

- *Do you model your principles? How?*

ACTION

- *Find an opportunity where you can share some of your personal values with your team.*

PRUNING

PRUNING DETERMINES THE number and position of the buds that develop on a vine. When the vine is young, the grower's interest centers on developing a single strong shoot having several well-placed laterals that will form a permanent framework. He sacrifices some of the plant's energy in order to obtain a well-shaped vine as cheaply and as early as possible.

Christopher took a semester-long viticulture class at Santa Rosa Junior College that focused on nothing but pruning. The entire class went from vineyard to vineyard on field trips to learn all the correct ways to prune. Because pruning has a depressing or stunting effect on the vine, it would be very easy to decrease the vine's total productivity through incorrect pruning techniques.

As an entrepreneur, you will face many difficult decisions in the building of your business, but knowing when and how to "prune" your staff will be one of the most difficult tasks you will face. Anyone who has had to fire an employee who is likable, obedient, and hardworking, but not competent enough to do the job well, will know what I mean.

In Captura's early days, we were so busy building the product that we did not focus on whether all the people were suited for their roles or for our company. Once we established our mission and our principles, we started to evaluate job roles and responsibilities. It became very clear that several people held similar expectations regarding their roles. Once we clearly defined our roles and responsibilities, we were able to start measuring performance.

Without walking through and pruning several other vineyards, my husband would not have been capable of pruning when it came time for him to perform that task in our vineyard. Even if you have developed job descriptions, recruited for positions, or fired someone, you will still face challenges in effectively managing your own business.

DISBUDDING YOUNG VINES

—∞—

IDENTIFYING THE PROBLEM

Young vines must be disbudded during their development. Disbudding consists of removing the swollen buds and young shoots from the lower part of the stem in order to concentrate the growth in one or more shoots which will be used to extend the trunk and develop branches or arms of the vine.

No matter how carefully you recruit, I guarantee that you will need to do some "disbudding" in the early stages of building your business. A start-up company is a unique business endeavor that is a bad match for a lot of people, and you may not know whether or not an individual is suitable until after he or she has joined the company. Even though you may have selected people for their skill or for their tenacity, integrity, and passion, that does not ensure that they will align with your principles as the business unfolds. The earlier you can identify those people who are a poor fit for your organization (because of attitude or aptitude), the quicker you can redirect the necessary energy to the remaining "vines."

We started with a handful of people at Captura and quickly expanded to nine full-time employees. By the end of the first year, three of those people had been "pruned" for the good of the team. As the leader, the difficult task of that pruning fell to me. It was difficult because all three were talented and good people whom I counted as my friends as well as co-founders.

The pruning method I have adopted is from the

leadership model of Jack Welch, CEO of General Electric. This model helps to determine where individual employees are in relation to results and shared values. Once you make these identifications, you can then take the appropriate action. Welch's model describes four types of employees:

- Type 1: These people meet and exceed performance goals *and* hold the company's mission and principles as sacred. They are the people you should support and promote.
- Type 2: These people miss performance goals *and* give lip service to the company values. They are in the wrong company and should be "pruned" as soon as possible.
- Type 3: These people miss performance goals, but hold the company's mission and principles as sacred. They need to be actively coached toward results or be moved to roles more suited to their skills. Failing that, they also should be pruned.
- Type 4: These people meet and exceed performance goals, but give lip service to the company mission and principles. They need to be actively coached on the principles. If there is no improvement, you will have to prune them.

I can't decide which is more difficult to prune —

type 3 or type 4. Both add value to a company, but if left in place without any changes, they will pull energy from the rest of the vine and you will regret not having taken action.

Midway through our vineyard's first fruit-bearing season, I came home to find my husband sitting in the dining room looking abjectly sad. When I inquired what was wrong, he said, "Didn't you notice the vineyard? I had to drop half of my crop today." Because the vines were so young and our soil so fertile, he had to cut back his crop in order to assure the quality of the remaining grapes. Even though it was the right decision, it was horrible for him to see mounds of clusters littering the ground. It doesn't feel any different when a leader has to let people go who are talented and bright, but not suited to their jobs.

Prune your business early and regularly. By doing so, you will assure the health and the proper growth of the organization.

QUESTIONS

- *Do you and your managers actively coach employees toward the company values?*

- Do you have employees that need to be "pruned"?

- Do you avoid the pruning task because it is unpleasant? If so, what price does your company pay for your inability to take action?

ACTION

- Review your staff against the Welch model. Create coaching plans for your type 3 and type 4 employees.

VIGOR AND CAPACITY

—⚋—

EXPANDING THE LEADERSHIP

Vigor and capacity are the two factors that a grower can control through training and pruning vines. Vigor is expressed by the vine's rate of growth. The more rapid the growth, the greater the vigor. Capacity is the total productive output of which the vine is potentially capable. The greater the total crop, the greater the capacity.

A young vine may show great vigor and yet have much less capacity than an older, mature vine. This was the case in our vineyard that first year; the vines were bearing too much fruit for their size, which is why Christopher had to cut back the crop. When a vine is young, the grower must take action to balance current growth against future capacity. If the vine puts too much energy into early growth, future productivity may be compromised. When your business starts to grow rapidly, you too will have to focus on both pruning and training. There will come a time when you will need to expand the leadership of the organization in order to support the company's growth. The faster you can train your management team, the better your chances of business success.

Given the unusual circumstances of my living arrangement (850 miles separate my home and my office) and my commitment to personal and professional balance, I had to come up with some creative ways to provide leadership to my company. I had made a commitment to my family to be home for at least three days each week. Because I do not travel on Sundays, I could only be in Seattle Monday afternoon through Thursday. In order to meet my needs and still provide the company with day-to-day leadership, I formed an Operating Committee during Captura's third year.

The four people who agreed to take on this responsibility represented all the functional areas of the company — sales and marketing, services, development, and finance. Each of these people had more than twenty years of business management experience. They knew the importance of modeling the company's mission and values. They understood how leaders model principles, how through clarity and courage of their convictions and everyday actions they demonstrate to others how visions can be realized. They also knew that they still had room to grow in their leadership and abilities. You may recall that one of our principles is that "we are committed to growth — our own and other people's." In taking on this new role, these people were challenging themselves to grow.

Their first task was to identify and publish their shared beliefs, philosophies, and principles. Over the course of YAO (Yet Another Off-site), they formulated their shared beliefs and translated them into principles. They also identified those areas of growth for themselves that would help them to succeed. During the course of their off-site work, they were challenged continually to "get out of their comfort zone" and stretch themselves in order to grow as fast as the company was growing.

In one exercise, they were given assignments challenging them to complete tasks that evening that were totally contrary to their personal behavioral styles. The VP of Sales and Marketing, who is a dynamic and verbal communicator, was asked to communicate only through pantomime all through dinner. The VP of Engineering, a logical and data-driven individual, was asked to tell a whimsical fantasy tale to the group after dinner. The VP of Services, who preferred thinking and planning over the actual nitty-gritty details of execution, had to cook and serve the dinner. And the CFO, whom I have nicknamed "Steady Eddie" because of his even temperament, was asked to write individual poems to be presented to each of us after dinner.

When they were given their assignments, you should have seen the looks of horror on their faces revealing how big a stretch they would be making to accomplish their tasks. What transpired over the next few hours was amazing to behold. By rising to these new challenges, they created a memorable evening of dining and entertainment for all of us.

To give you an example, with the author's permission, I am reprinting the poem that my CFO wrote for me. As you read this, remember that this is a man who tallies numbers for a living.

FACETS OF DANA
by Bob Colliton

Dana,
You are a multifaceted person,
a prism,
capturing your vision as a beam of light,
redirecting that light in new directions,
at times, reflecting one color more dominantly than
    the other,
red — the passionate visionary and CEO

blue — the jazz musician and drummer
yellow — the eternal optimist, continually striving
*   to find the good in each situation*
green — the nurturing mother, teacher and gar-
*   dener, planting seeds of new ideas, innovation*
and challenge, while challenging yourself as well
strong and dominant colors striving for
balance and harmony
reflecting a rainbow.

Is it any wonder that I believe in the potential of each and every person to achieve greatness? I believe that if you give people the environment and the chance to grow, they will amaze you with what they accomplish. I will cherish my poem forever because it came from the purely good intention of someone's heart.

Over the next year, these leaders were faced with managing 200 percent growth in our staff and 1,000 percent growth in our customer base. They had to overcome financial hurdles, operational obstacles, and product deficiencies, while keeping the company running smoothly. That they were able to do so is a testimony to their belief in team and their adherence to their principles.

QUESTIONS

- *Have you identified the strong leaders underneath you?*

- *What are you doing to assist their growth?*

- *Are you actively delegating leadership tasks to others. Why why not?*

ACTION

- *Create a written plan of succession for your role as owner/founder.*

IRRIGATION

FOR MAXIMUM PRODUCTIVITY, California vineyards require from 16 to 54 inches of available water, depending on climate, soil, grape variety, and the slope of the land. In commercial vineyards, regardless of location, supplemental irrigation is practiced everywhere that water is available, in order to maximize the yield of the vineyard. Even in the cool coastal valleys of California, where soils may hold twelve inches or more of readily available water within the root zone, supplemental irrigation is used to increase productivity.

Just as a vineyard requires water, a business requires money. Passion does not pay the bills. Vision does not allow you to expand your staff. And going broke with your principles intact is not a worthwhile goal. Money is the necessary ingredient for making your dreams a reality. Like all the other steps in building a business, its acquisition and application require a well-thought-out and well-executed plan.

Although our property had been a vineyard many decades earlier, it had never been irrigated. The previous growers had "dry-farmed" the land. Because the soil could hold plenty of rainwater, they had chosen not to irrigate. Under such conditions, the vines had grown well, produced good crops, and kept their leaves until frost. When water supplies are limited, vines adjust by ceasing growth early, bearing small crops, and dropping their leaves in late summer. Obviously, in such cases, the crops are not as large as they could be with additional water.

Once Christopher decided on Syrah as his grape of choice, he immediately began investigating our well's capacity and various irrigation systems. After months of research, he decided on an underground drip system, a relatively new way of irrigating a vineyard. It took the entire first year to retrofit our well to enable it to support 3,000 vines and to dig and lay and test the miles of underground hose. Because fertilizer could be pushed through the drip system, thus applying nutrients directly to the roots, Christopher was able to have a crop in the second year, a year earlier than usual. The yield he can now generate is ten tons per acre, in contrast to one to two tons per acre on dry-farmed property. His choice of irrigation has definitely paid off.

As I mentioned in the introduction, I had the good fortune of being able to start my business endeavor with my own cash and the investments of the other founders. It was not nearly enough, however, to build an enterprise software company, which averages $15 million in investment before profitability.

Therefore, I had to face the challenges and financial stress involved in keeping a business running without capital or revenue. Having already experienced financial failure earlier in my life when I built a different business, it was a "déjà vu" experience I would happily have foregone. But, as with all difficult situations, I learned so many valuable lessons that I am actually grateful for the experience. I hope reading about my struggle will help you avoid one of your own.

How Soils are Wetted

—⁓—

The Venture Capital World

Water is available through rainfall or in the water tables; unfortunately, working capital is not so easily and readily accessible. Whether through formal or informal channels, you will find yourself confronting venture capitalists. My guess is that the term "venture capital" arose from the phrase "backing a venture" or from the "nothing ventured, nothing gained" school of thought. Venture capital is the money available to be put at risk to help an entrepreneur build a business. It is not a loan nor does it require collateral. Venture capital comes from many sources — family, friends, employees, employees' families, former employers, acquaintances, friends of friends, friends of friends of acquaintances . . . you get the picture.

Captura has investors from every one of those categories. There was a period of six to nine months when all I did was chase down any lead for any potential private investor. In increments of $25,000, I raised more than $2 million. Much of it came from the employees and founders (not that they could afford it), but a fair amount of investment came from other folks as well. It's a lot of work to raise money privately in this fashion, but I did not have a choice. I had no experience in the formal world of venture capital, and it took a while to educate myself on how venture capitalists operate and where to find them. A few tips:

- Venture capital is not found at the bank.
- Venture capital firms are looking for high return on their investments.
- Venture capital firms are not blind risk takers; they are calculated risk takers.
- Venture capital firms vary greatly in attitude and philosophy.

- Without a solid business proposal, venture capitalists will not be interested.

The World Wide Web has made locating everything easier, including venture capital. Most firms have their own web sites detailing the types of investments they look for, the size of their fund, and profiles of their partners.

Two published lists are available to help you in your search for the right venture capital company for your situation. The first contains the names of firms licensed by the Small Business Administration. These are the most active venture capital companies. If you want a comprehensive listing, check out the web site at www.nasbic.org or write to:

National Association of Small Business Investment Companies
1666 11th St. N.W.
Suite 750
Washington, D.C. 20001
Phone (202) 628-5055
Fax (202) 628-5080

The second list is of the members of a trade association of venture capitalists not affiliated with the government. A current list can be obtained at their web site at www.nvca.org or by writing to:

The National Venture Capital Association

1655 North Fort Myer Dr., Suite 700

Arlington, VA 22209

Phone (703) 524-2549

Fax (703) 524-3940

A venture capitalist wants to back a unique business that will produce a high return for the investors. Many venture capitalists consider management to be the key to successful ventures, and they will take a hard look at your experience, as well as that of the other key members of your team. Financial projections and exit strategy (the means by which they will receive a return on their investment) will also be key factors influencing their decision to invest. All these factors must be presented in a succinct summary backed up with a strong proposal.

In general, the topics you should cover in your business proposal are:

- What — the business and its future
- Why — the market potential, the barriers to entry, and the competitive landscape
- Who — the management team and their backgrounds and experience
- How — the analysis of projections and operations and the distribution plan

- How Much — a description of the financing, return on investment and exit and financial statements

Your business proposal's most important characteristics are clarity and conciseness. The final product should be thirty to forty pages. The first business plan I shopped to venture capitalists was more than 150 pages. After getting some advice from professionals, the next one I submitted was less than thirty, including the projections. That plan was the one that resulted in funding.

Keep it simple and address the main ideas important to a venture capitalist — the uniqueness of your proposal, the experience of you and your team, and the potential for high return on investment.

QUESTIONS

- *What do you think is the value of your company? Why?*

- *Would you let your family and friends invest in your company? Why or why not?*

- *Do you have a complete business plan? Why or why not?*

Actions

- *Create a business proposal.*

- *Review the web sites of at least three venture capital firms that specialize in your industry.*

- *Call the CEOs of some of the firms that are funded and get firsthand advice on what the venture capitalists who backed them are looking for in an investment.*

- *Find a coach who knows how to raise capital. Hire him to help you through this phase of growing your business.*

INSUFFICIENT MOISTURE

—〰—

DETERMINING THE NEED FOR CAPITAL

An abrupt and severe reduction in the water supply to a growing vine causes wilting of the leaves and succulent shoots. A restricted supply of water, depriving part but not all of the root zone, causes characteristic symptoms that an experienced grower readily recognizes. A change in appearance and the shortening of the actively growing tips are accompanied by the drying-up of the tendrils at the shoot tips.

Once Christopher had our vines in the ground and the irrigation in place, he thought the growth of his crop was assured. Only days after turning on the drip system, however, he discovered that our well was "sucking sand" in its efforts to keep up with the increased demand of all the irrigation under way. Experts were immediately called upon to help correct the problem. In the meantime, Christopher had to rotate the water among the rows. Not until months later, when all systems were working, did he discover that several sections had received no water during the crucial growing months. To this day, those sections remain the least robust of our entire vineyard and a constant reminder of what lack of moisture can do to a crop.

Likewise, lack of money can bring on sieges of anxiety, despair, and negativism, the effects of which may be felt for a long time. When our initial capital ran out in 1996, I sent proposals to more than thirty venture capital firms. I met with the representatives of five firms and was turned down each time. The reasons ranged from "We do not think there is a market for your product" (the actual verbatim quote: "There is no dog for your dog food") to "Come back when you have customers" to "We don't believe you can do it." It was the most discouraging experience I have ever had. Months of severe frustration followed. Clearly, our success hinged on penetrating the venture capital world. After twelve months, though, I had made zero progress.

The Civil War general Thomas "Stonewall" Jackson advised, "Never take counsel with your fears." It was good that I didn't, because we had no money, no customers, and no prospects. My financial plight was such that I was living hand-to-mouth. I borrowed and wheedled, fretted and worried, and somehow managed. As I have said, starting your own business requires more than a fair amount of courage and tenacity.

After all the rejections, it became agonizingly clear

to me that the rude rebuffs I was receiving indicated a flaw in my business plan. As a result, I toiled day after day to educate myself about marketing and sales so that I could devise a compelling business proposal. I focused less on raising money and more on running the business and keeping creditors at bay while I tried to sell my product. I figured the best way to convince investors that we were a viable company was to have customers and revenue.

When we had no irrigation in our vineyard, we literally hand-watered those areas most in need. At Captura, I used the same premise. I asked the staff to determine minimum cash requirements; each month, I endeavored to meet those needs through borrowing or "begging" for the money from existing investors or from the bank. One of our investors, Scott, runs his own small consulting business with its own cash-flow concerns. But when he realized we were not going to make payroll one month, he showed up in my office in gangster get-up with a briefcase holding $25,000 in cash. He brought humor and lightness to a weary and burdened staff. Only later did I learn that he had borrowed against his personal line of credit to get that money.

If I had done my homework on the amount of capital the company really would need to get its product to market, I could have done a much better job of raising the money in an orderly and professional manner. If I had done my homework, I could have avoided the unpleasant effects that a lack of capital incurs.

QUESTIONS

- *Do you know how much money you will need to grow your business?*

- *Do you have a plan for getting that capital?*

- *Has your coach validated your plan?*

- *Do you have a back-up strategy if your projections turn out to be incorrect?*

ACTION

- *Review your financial projections with other industry sources who can affirm or refute your assumptions and projections and bring overlooked items to your attention.*

VINE RESPONSES TO SOIL MOISTURE CONDITIONS
—∿—
FACING FAILURE

In a vineyard, insufficient water during the early period of rapid berry enlargement prevents the attainment of normal berry size. Applying water after this period of growth is past will not enable the undersized berries to reach normal size. A severe shortage of readily available water during ripening delays maturity, gives the fruit a dull color, and often allows sunburn.

Obviously, my inability to fund Captura affected my husband's ability to keep the vineyard development under way. As our entire personal savings had been depleted through investment in both Captura and the vineyard, neither of us could continue providing the necessary "water" to our respective crops. While I struggled to control the fears dominating my thoughts, Christopher struggled to work on his irrigation system without the assistance of the vineyard management firm, which we could no longer afford to hire. Time and again, we discussed whether we should just give up and call it quits. In those dark days, it seemed there would never be a crop or a Captura customer. Suddenly, the prospect of failure seemed all too likely.

On a plane trip to Seattle during this time, I listened to a conversation between an older businessman and a young woman about to embark on her career whom he was counseling about those factors that he felt were most important for success. "Believe in yourself," he told her. "Find a mentor who can show you the ropes. Commit to follow that person's instruction. Never stop learning or trying to better yourself, and you will find your job a joy."

At the end of the flight, I couldn't help but let him know that I had overheard him and appreciated his words of wisdom. He asked me what I did, and I told him about Captura. It turned out he was a vice president with Merrill Lynch. We traded business cards, and within weeks Captura was invited to respond to Merrill Lynch's request for information about our product. Three months later, we signed a "try before you buy" deal. Captura finally had its first big customer!

Months of effort from many people were required to customize our product in order to meet Merrill Lynch's complex needs, but in doing so we created a better product and a high-value relationship, and we were able to keep the business running.

In the meantime, Christopher persuaded the winemaker at Geyser Peak Winery that his crop of Syrah would be of superior quality and well suited to making Shiraz. He signed a contract with the winery and convinced it to give him fifty percent of the payment for his crop up front, allowing him to keep farming the land properly while awaiting the harvest.

I have often reflected on those events that helped us turn a corner, and I would like to share the conclusions I reached based upon how events unfolded at Captura and at Bruttig Vineyards:

- New possibilities and opportunities await you every day, but you must pursue them. What if I had remained silent on that plane trip?

- An unwavering belief in yourself is necessary if you are going to hold on through the dark days. What if Christopher had failed to convince Geyser Peak of the value of his yet-to-appear crop?

- A support system of people who believe in you is crucial to your ability to face failure and keep going. If I had stayed at home dwelling on my predicament, I would never have taken that fateful plane trip.

One entrepreneur whom I admire for his courage and willingness to overcome the likelihood of failure is

John H. Johnson, the founder of *Ebony* magazine. While he continually butted his head against the wall of racial prejudice, he refused to fail. "When I see a barrier, I cry and I curse, and then I get a ladder and climb over it," he said.

You must have your ladder ready in order to climb over all the barriers awaiting you.

QUESTIONS

- *Have you ever failed? How did you respond?*

- *What is the worst thing that could happen if your business failed?*

- *Have you known others who have faced failure? What did you notice about them as they went through the ordeal?*

- *Who can you turn to in your darkest moments of doubt?*

ACTIONS

- *List all the "undiscussable" thoughts you have about the failure of your business. Share them with someone.*

- *Look for opportunities and new possibilities whenever you get stuck.*

Notes

NOTES

THE POWER OF PERSEVERANCE

Just like moons and like suns,
With the certainty of tides,
Just like hopes springing high,
Still I'll rise.

— Maya Angelou

CULTIVATION

IN AGRICULTURE, THE term "cultivation" is most commonly applied to the loosening, turning, or stirring of the soil around and between growing plants. In vineyards, it includes all the various manipulations of the soil after the vines have been planted.

Cultivation is practiced in some form in most commercial vineyards. Frequency and depth vary widely. The general purposes of vineyard cultivation are: to destroy weeds; to facilitate such vineyard operations as irrigation and harvesting; to prepare the soil for cover crops; to incorporate cover crops and fertilizers into the soil; to help control certain pests; and to promote the absorption of water.

In our vineyard, Christopher regularly disks the soil between the rows of vines and sprays regularly in order to keep the weeds around the vines from choking off nutrition. He must be extremely careful when performing both activities. When turning the soil, he could accidentally sever a drip line lying just below the surface, thereby cutting off nutrients to the vines. When spraying, he must take care not to get any of the chemicals on the leaves, which would harm the vine itself.

At Captura, we cultivated our company through the sale of our product to Merrill Lynch and EG&G. This helped facilitate our efforts to raise capital. But we also had to take care that, as we worked with these companies, we avoided dedicating all our sales and service efforts toward them. If we did, we would be unable to leverage our product development efforts and build the business by selling the product to several hundred other customers.

We had to balance our disking and spraying.

There are also "weeds" that will grow in your business. At Captura, we had to control the effect of new employees and outside investors so that they would not "overrun" our tender young vines. It is often easy to get so caught up with solving an immediate problem that you overlook the possible long-term effects that may result from your decision. If you remember that your root system is your strength, you will be better able to combat all the weeds that try to take over your vines.

TILLAGE IMPLEMENTS

—∞—

GETTING ASSISTANCE

Useful in cultivating between the rows of vines are plows, disks, harrows, and plank or steel drags. The choice of tools is governed by the nature of the soil, the power available for pulling the implements, the distance between the rows, the nature of the cover crops, and the preference of the operator.

When Christopher began planning his vineyard, he immediately purchased a tractor. Even before our purchase of the property had closed, we were the proud owners of a 1948 Ford 8N tractor, complete with scraper, bucket, auger, and disker. Christopher was on that tractor almost daily for two years — moving trees, digging holes, and turning soil. It was an indispensable tool in establishing the vineyard.

When I started Captura, one of my recruits was a man with marketing expertise. Unfortunately, his tenure with the company was brief, and I did not replace him. I thought we could get by without a "marketeer" until we had a product to sell. Was I mistaken! If I had the chance to do one single thing differently, I would bring on a marketing person much earlier than I did.

In any event, once we signed Merrill Lynch, I finally knew I needed a "tractor" in order to cultivate my land. I found it in Katarina, a woman who is definitely a TIPster. She has an abundance of enthusiasm and brilliance to go along with her tenacity, integrity, and passion. With a background in sales and marketing, she brought a new perspective to the company. When she first joined us, I finally had a signed term sheet from a venture capital firm on the East Coast for an investment in the company. Although the terms were not the best (for Captura) and I did not like the firm, I was in no position to turn it down.

Unfortunately, we did not have the deal closed in time to make payroll that month, so Katarina decided to invest in the company and thereby paid herself the first month she was here. What a way to demonstrate commitment!

A month after Katarina joined, we were undergoing the last stages of "due diligence," the process whereby a venture capital firm examines a company's documents and financial status. Associates from this particular venture capital firm came to our offices to review all our documents. While using my office, they came upon a copy of my personal development plan which had been filed securely in my desk drawer (or so I thought). In that plan, I had outlined my three-month, six-month, and one-year goals for myself. Besides personal items such as weight loss and fitness goals, it also included the goals for my role as CEO. I was planning to redefine my role so that I would be less involved in operations and more involved in the promotion and vision of the company.

The next day, I received a very heated call from the partners at the venture capital firm. They demanded that I fly east immediately in order to discuss this document. They demanded that Katarina come as well. They were not sure that they could invest in Captura after all, if I was planning to leave. No amount of explanation over the phone could dissuade them.

I felt that if they backed out, Captura would be finished.

Katarina and I went to the "inquisition" (as we call it now) where we were separated and questioned about our commitment to the company. It was horrible. After we were done, I returned to my hotel room and cried. I thought for sure that we were finished. It was almost a good feeling — at last we could quit. I could escape from this ordeal. Then I thought about Corey, Joe, Jeffrey, Jennifer, John, and all the people who had worked so hard for the Captura dream, and I knew I had to persevere.

The venture capital firm did indeed decide not to invest in Captura after all.

I flew home the next day and started evaluating our cash situation. It looked dire. We had piles of debts and, now that the money we had been counting on wasn't forthcoming, it was only a matter of time before our creditors got ugly. On the bright side, however, our customers loved the product and the implementations were going well. We had just signed two new customers and reached an OEM (Original Equipment Manufacturer) agreement with Carlson Wagonlit Tavel, a national travel agency, whereby it would market our product under its own label.

I negotiated an agreement with our bank whereby it would loan us money against our invoices if our customers provided verification. We had an invoice outstanding with Merrill Lynch, so with much trepidation (who wants to let on, expecially to a customer, that they're broke?), I called Merrill Lynch's vice president of investment banking to ask if she would verify the invoice. She readily agreed, and I hung up the phone and thought, "Well, at least that will give me some time to figure out what to do."

In that moment, I did something I had never done before. I surrendered. I acknowledged that the situation was out of my hands and that I had done the best I could. In doing so, I was finally able to accept that whatever would be, would be. The weight lifted, and I sat there smiling.

Then the phone rang. It was the VP from Merrill Lynch calling back. She said, "Dana, after I hung up, I realized you must be having cash-flow problems if you need to borrow from the bank. I was wondering, can we help?"

I was speechless.

She went on, "We love your product, and we have a fund that invests in small companies like yours. Would you be interested in having us as an investor?"

After picking myself up off the floor, I mumbled something resembling affirmation, hung up the phone, and cried, this time from sheer joy and relief.

What I learned from this painful experience was that the assistance you need may be right under your nose — that employee with a skill set you didn't realize he had, that friend who always wanted to program software, or that customer who could invest in the company. I also learned that "giving up" can be the best thing you can do for yourself and your company. I think that, as entrepreneurs, we sometimes take on so much responsibility that it clouds our vision and prevents us from seeing clearly what is right in front of us. Don't be so sure about how something should look that you miss recognizing when something better comes along.

One of my favorite singers, Barbra Streisand, was fixated on becoming an actress and filmmaker from a very young age. She poured all her efforts into her dream and got nowhere. Only when someone heard her sing at home and compliment her did she realize that her unique voice was what she had to offer the world of entertainment. What a lucky thing for all of us that Streisand's energy was redirected toward music.

QUESTIONS

- *What resources do you have available that you may be overlooking?*

- *Do you ever allow yourself to "surrender"? Why or why not?*

- *How do you get assistance when you need it?*

ACTION

- *Make a list of all the resources available to you (people, talents, money, equipment, etc.). Create a thirty-day action plan that will allow you to access all these resources to assist you or your business.*

WEED CONTROL

—∿—

PROTECTING YOUR PRINCIPLES

Weeds must be kept under control. In a vineyard, control means complete elimination soon after the winter rains are over, before the weeds have robbed the soil of moisture needed to carry the vines through the summer. Following that, weeds need to be kept in check sufficiently so that they do not gobble up soil nutrients or interfere with such operations as pest control and harvesting.

In our vineyard, we use chemicals to control the weeds. Because we have such a perfect climate for growing grapes, we also have perfect climate for growing weeds. If we did not spray regularly during the spring and summer, we would have weeds literally over our heads. Keeping them in check is a constant battle, which is why I can remember, day after day, seeing Christopher and his tractor going back and forth endlessly between the vines.

At Captura, I felt as though I had been running my own tractor up and down the rows. Just keeping the creditors at bay was a full-time job. And, as many small companies do, we got behind with the nastiest weed of all — the government taxing authority. We owed back payroll taxes, and I had been working diligently with my local IRS agent, Ken, on a payment plan, as well as keeping him up-to-date on our funding activities. I have to say that the IRS was more than accommodating in those first few months, but as the situation dragged on and on, relations got a little tense.

Now, I know I have said a lot of positive things about the value of perseverance in achieving your dreams, but weariness can and does overtake the best of us. In my case, when I am weary, I tend to lose my ability to reason.

After Merrill Lynch agreed to invest the same amount that we had hoped to receive from the East Coast venture capital firm ($2.5 million), we immediately began the process of due diligence. We were eager (as were my friends at the IRS) to get the paperwork done so that we could get the money in the bank. As one month dragged into two and then three, I began to run out of things to tell my buddy, Ken the IRS man. Although he had nicely put off taking any legal action, I think his patience finally wore out when I informed him of yet another delay. He was ready to file a lien, as well as a 100 percent penalty, against me personally.

I crumbled.

All I could see were the years it would take me to pay off the amounts he was throwing out. I got him to promise to give me three days before taking action, and I went into "panic mode."

I called my attorneys, told them the situation, and asked if they thought we could get the funding done by the end of the week (we were four weeks past the original closing date). They went to work with Merrill Lynch's legal firm to see if they could accelerate things.

Then I placed a call to a local investment bank that had assisted me in getting other bridge loans in the past to see if its people could help out. They also went to work.

Within 48 hours, I had some answers. I could get an immediate investment from a private individual to cover the taxes, but the amount of stock we would have to give up would jeopardize the $2.5 million from Merrill Lynch. I decided that in order to protect my family, I had to take the offer (the proverbial bird in the hand). I was devastated that we would once again have to seek additional funding, but I couldn't see any other solution to my predicament. I called Merrill Lynch's investment banker, Steve, to let him know we could not complete the financing. All along, Steve had been an

advocate of Captura and had been tremendously helpful in getting the investment committee to approve the
investment. In the scheme of things, our $2.5 million
was a relatively small amount for an investor the size of
Merrill Lynch. I expected that I wouldn't hear back.

At home that night, I received a call from Steve. He
was angry and disappointed that I was "backing out." I
explained the circumstances behind my decision. Remember, at this point I was very weary. In a thoughtful
and evenhanded way, he began to talk with me about
my principles. He reminded me that this was not about
me, but about the team. He wanted to know if I really
believed this decision was in Captura's best interests.
He reminded me that our mission statement says we
"create and sustain high-value relationships," and he
made me see that Merrill Lynch was a much more high-
value relationship than any other I could undertake.

I am forever beholden to Steve's willingness to work
with me that night. He made me see what I needed to
see. He helped me overcome the fear that was leading
me to make a poor decision for my company.

By reconnecting with my principles, I overcame my
"temporary insanity" and was able to make a decision
that has resulted in continued growth and prosperity
for Captura. I did not do it alone, however. I believe that

sometimes there are "angels" in our lives who remind us of what we know but have temporarily forgotten. Steve was that kind of angel for me.

Of course, I stuck with Merrill Lynch after that conversation, and its representatives scrambled to advance me the monies to pay the IRS and to close the financing within two weeks. Since that time, they have invested another $2 million in Captura and were instrumental in introducing me to my venture capital firms, Oak Investment Partners and Voyager Capital.

My experience with Oak Investment Partners and Voyager Capital was in direct contrast to the situation with the East Coast venture capital firm. The partner from Oak who sits on my board, Fred, is a man of high integrity and brilliant business insight. He provides exactly what venture capitalists say they will: contacts, guidance, and support without interference. Voyager's representative, Tony, has assisted with the acquisition of a local company and has given good advice over Tuesday-night beers at Canyon's restaurant. They both are stellar examples of the value (besides money) that venture capitalists can provide to an entrepreneur. If a venture capital firm doesn't feel like a good match or if it doesn't embrace your principles, *don't* take its money. The weeds will overwhelm you.

Questions

- *What principles do you hold as non-negotiable?*

- *When you are under stress, how do you react?*

- *Can you identify an "angel" in your life who helps you stay connected with your principles and your higher purpose?*

Action

- *Find those principles defined in your personal mission statement that can assist you in times of stress. Put them in front of you on your desk.*

Stages of Berry Development

—∿∿—

Managing Change

As the berries increase in size, they pass through several stages of development from the time of setting until full ripeness. The changes in the fruit, though continuous, proceed at different rates during different stages. So it is with change in business; it can happen slowly and unnoticed, or with great and sudden impact, or somewhere in between.

Once Christopher had the well working, the underground drip system fixed, and the weeds under control, his hands-on activities in the vineyard decreased. Now, it was the sun that became the catalyst for growth.

Likewise, once Captura was funded, we were able to hire additional staff in order to market and sell the product, which allowed the company to grow without my personal efforts being so essential to the process.

In viticulture, the "green stage" extends from the time the berries set until they begin to ripen. During this period, the main change is rapid increase in berry size. At Captura, we tripled staff within six months. We changed from an intimate group of people who had shared the rigors of starting a company to an assembly of professionals who were expanding on these earlier efforts to develop a market-leading company.

This early stage of growth was marked by the following challenges:

- Conveying the idea that each individual needed to "play his position." After years of "beehive soccer" where *everyone* was involved in *everything*, there was a need for a transition in roles and responsibilities. This was a difficult change for many of the founding employees.
- Expanding the service side of the business in order to deal with a growing customer base.
- Managing remote employees located in the newly created field offices.

These challenges were met by continued recruitment of new managers with expertise in sales, service, and formal product development. In order to keep the principles of Captura intact in the midst of all the growth, we introduced management training seminars based upon the Covey principles.

I also instituted a monthly luncheon for new employees. Following the meal at these functions, the employees share collages representing themselves — their histories, their values, their lives. Through the years, these "self-portraits" have become more and more in-novative; many now adorn the walls of the company, reflecting the uniqueness of the individuals who make up Captura.

QUESTIONS

- *Do you a formal way of welcoming new employees?*

- *How do new employees get to know the mission and principles of your company?*

ACTION

- *Create your own collage portrait to share with your employees.*

HARVESTING

IF YOU HAVE NEVER had the pleasure of visiting a wine region during the "crush," you have really missed out on one of life's best events. After all the hard work of establishing a vineyard, cultivating the land, and nurturing the young vines through the first years, everything culminates in the harvest. It is a truly magical time when the whole valley smells of fermenting grapes, and the crisp, cool air carries the sound of the frenetic movement of trucks and farmworkers traveling rapidly from vineyard to vineyard.

Wine grapes in California are harvested at a single picking. Maturity must therefore be gauged as precisely as possible — the accuracy of this decision largely determines the quality of the product, within the limits or possibilities of the particular variety. The finer the variety, the more important is proper maturity. A wine grape is ripe when it reaches a chemical and physical composition that, given the environment in which it was cultivated, is the optimum for the particular wine for which it is intended.

The first year Christopher made wine, it was from grapes he purchased, since our vineyard was still under construction. He faithfully took samples weekly in August and then daily in September, until the magical day when he called for the picking. I was trying to coordinate a "harvest party" with friends and family and found it quite annoying that it was impossible to predict the exact day when we would be picking. I have since learned that you can party even though the grapes are not ready!

Although Christopher's winemaking endeavors that first year were worthy of a bronze medal at the California State Fair, he was still eager to see what kind of wine his own crop would produce.

Likewise at Captura, although we had a product, capital, and customers, we were still excited about our company's opportunities for growth. We started developing new products and enhancing our original one.

Vineyard Sampling

—∞—

Walk-Around Management

The ripening stage starts with the development of color and ends when the fruit has reached a composition that is ideally suited for the wine for which it will be used. The winemaker determines exactly when the grapes are ripe based upon samples taken during the ripening stage.

Because the causes of variability in the composition of fruit are so numerous, maturity must be tested in all parts of the vineyard. Christopher will take ten to twenty clusters from throughout the vineyard and combine them for testing. The most significant criteria of wine grape maturity are sugar content, acidity, pH, and Balling-acid ratio of freshly expressed juice.

Likewise, in your business, you must constantly take samples of the organization's "ripeness." Once sales went up at Captura, the pressure on the development staff increased as well. Suddenly, the product was being utilized in ways we had neither the resources nor the time to test and verify. The inevitable "bug" database began to grow. There were new stresses on the organization, such as training new employees while continuing to be productive. We all received paychecks now, but the rapid rate of change was causing as much stress as had earlier financial instability.

As the leader of the organization, it falls to you to monitor and manage your company's dynamics. As your firm grows, you will be required to understand and implement management techniques that will assure smooth operation of the business. One of saddest days at Captura was when we developed our Employee Handbook and the dreaded Organizational Chart. I still can't stand either, but I know both are necessary for managing growth. It was sad because it signaled the end of the entrepreneurial "anything goes" days when everyone would do whatever was necessary for the business. When you add employees, however, you also must add rules and policies.

Typically, there are two types of people in a start-up organization — the producers and the supporters. As an entrepreneur, you are most likely a producer. Entrepreneurs are founders of companies and innovators of new concepts. Usually, they are not suited for supportive, operational roles. For the benefit of the business, however, most entrepreneurs learn to broaden their skill set to include management. Once your company exceeds fifty employees, though, you need to consider expanding your management team to include people who can implement systems that produce and measure results.

Each division leader at Captura is responsible for the timely creation and presentation of a detailed Operational Plan every quarter. These plans are part of the controls for my organization. They outline specific divisional performance goals and the tasks and time-frames necessary to achieve the goals. As the chief executive, you will need a steady flow of information in order to form an accurate picture of the company's performance. On our company IntraNet, we have a "dashboard" that is updated weekly to show the key business indicators. I can go there to see current financial numbers, sales prospects, and customer updates. To really know how the company is doing, however, I do what Christopher does in his vineyard — I walk the rows and look at the vines.

I take time to walk around and chat with my employees. The larger your organization, the further out of touch you will get from front-line troops. Initially, you have extensive worker input; as the company grows, you lose that input. Although solid numerical data is the key to good management, you should never neglect the opportunity to listen to your employees and customers. This anecdotal information is critical to keeping your finger on the pulse of your company. It will help you identify needed improvements, problem areas, and significant opportunities. With all that is required of you in managing a fast-growing company, it is easy to forget to take the time to connect with the people. If you don't, though, you will not have all the information necessary to make the best decisions.

Walk around and stop by a cubicle to see what someone is working on. Attend a project team meeting to catch up on a product's status. Form employee groups charged with giving you feedback on specific areas of the company. At Captura, these groups are called "task forces," and they have been instrumental in devising new ways to develop products, recruit employees, and serve customers.

Your success at this phase of your company's growth will rely less on your skills as a producer and more on your abilities as a promoter. You must develop a talent for selecting, recruiting, training, and inspiring department heads.

QUESTIONS

- *Who have you given the responsibility of managing the operational elements of your business?*

- *From what sources do you gather the data you need to make appropriate business decisions?*

- *How much time do you spend with your employees?*

ACTION

- *Create employee feedback groups charged with providing you with input.*

Time to Harvest

—⚏—

One Milestone of Many

If you have made it through the excitement of planning and layout, the difficulty of planting and weeding, the hope of the first buds, and the despair of early frost, you are then more than ready for the harvest. I will warn you that, rather than the emotional high you expect, you will more likely experience deep gratitude to be participating in this important step of the journey.

I will always remember our vineyard's first harvest because of all it represented. After the years of hard work and the patient waiting for the exact moment when we would see our grapes picked and thrown into a crusher, the harvest itself was quick and anticlimactic. Because there is only a small yield the first year a crop is ready, we did not have much to harvest. The vineyard workers descended on our property in the early morning. With the precision and speed of those who are skilled at their task, they left our vineyard bare by the end of the day. Only when we saw the grapes go into the crusher to begin the journey to becoming wine did we realize that we were just one part of a larger process. The harvest was just one milestone of many. We had not reached our destination after all, but merely a moment to reflect on where we had been, where we were now, and where we were going. Many more harvests would come and go, but that first one will remain documented by photographs on our walls and videos in our cabinet, because it represented a dream come alive.

In the same way, the "harvest" at Captura was significant. After closing our initial round of funding with $2.5 million, our next round's target was $7 million. By that time, we had many customers and were finally producing healthy revenue. In meetings with several venture capital firms, I had my choice of whom I wanted as investors. Many of the firms that had turned me down a year earlier were now pounding on my door trying to convince me they should be my investors. I settled on Oak Investment Partners and Voyager Capital for all the reasons I mentioned earlier.

The actual signing of documents and transfer of funds was as anticlimactic as the vineyard's first harvest, but I keep the documents framed in my office for the same reason I keep the pictures in Healdsburg.

Questions

- *Do you take time to reflect on where you have been and where you are going?*

- *Do you acknowledge the milestones of your business growth?*

- *What are the biggest milestones ahead of you?*

Action

- *Make a plan to hold an event (for example, a dinner, a champagne and cake meeting, or a company picnic) to acknowledge your next business milestone.*

HARVESTING PROCEDURE

—∿—

THE IMPORTANCE OF ACKNOWLEDGMENT

Following is the text of a speech I gave at a dinner held on August 15, 1997. In attendance were employees, spouses, investors, board members, and other people who had helped in Captura's development and success, gathered together that evening to raise a glass to our milestone. I am reprinting it here to permanently acknowledge those people who contributed to Captura.

Almost a year ago, recognizing that we were in the midst of uncertainty about our future, I arranged an all-employee off-site. We went to Healdsburg, in the wine country, for the harvest. The focus of the off-site was on abundance and prosperity. We discussed what it took for healthy growth; we discussed the vines, the soil, the weather, the trellis systems, the fertilizing, and the water. We spent a full day actually picking Petite Sirah and Carignane grapes for Bruttig Vineyards. And while that activity gave us an appreciation *for all that went into healthy growth, the year since then has given Captura the experience of what actually goes into the growth of a company.*

We have learned firsthand what is expressed so eloquently in the following quote by Teddy Roosevelt, which I would like to share with you:

"It is not the critic who counts; not the man who points out how the strong man stumbles, or where the doer of deeds could have done them better. The credit belongs to the man in the arena, whose face is marred by dust and sweat and blood; who strives valiantly; who knows the great enthusiasms, the great devotions; who spends himself in a worthy cause; who at the best knows in the end the triumph of high achievement and who at the worst, if he fails, at least fails while daring greatly, so that his place shall never be with those cold and timid souls who have never known either victory or defeat."

We now know what it is to be the "man in the arena," what is really necessary for growth. We know intimately the feel of dust and blood and sweat. Being in the "arena" has exacted a price, not only financially, but also to our personal relationships and to our physical well-being.

Without the support of our families, our friends, and our significant others, I am convinced we would not be here today. So, to those of you here tonight who stood by your loved ones as they came home many a late night and kept promising month after month that things would get better and paychecks really were part of working at Captura, we all want to sincerely thank you for your encouragement, your belief, and your commitment to all of us who were in the arena, striving valiantly. The credit goes to you as well. And to those of you who have elected to join us in the arena, we welcome you and remind you that if you too stay in the arena, the triumph of high achievement also awaits you.

As I look at the Captura that exists today, I cannot help but see a beautiful mosaic made up of many, many unique stones. And as I have examined these stones, I have come to appreciate how necessary each and every one was in creating the powerful picture we now have. And I ask myself, "What would Captura be without this stone or that stone?"

What would Captura be without:

- *The idea for automating T&E — thank you,*

Gerald Blackie.

- *PAWFS and RASL and DASL — thank you, Corey Mandell.*
- *The touch algorithm and credit card integration — thank you, Jeffrey Keyes.*
- *Its register look and its standard user interface — thank you, Joe Pacquette.*
- *CapMail — thank you, Alan Buck.*
- *EG&G, its first paying customer — thank you, Bill Falk.*
- *Rosenbluth, its first OEM contract — thank you, Jennifer Starbuck.*
- *Its user guide and web site — thank you, Audryn Webb.*
- *Littlejohn, BigBob, and RAS — thank you, Jason Boyle.*
- *Per diem and referenceable customers — thank you, Jim Phelps.*
- *Gilligan and professor test scripts — thank you, Jim Conley.*
- *Company car — thank you, Scott Klein.*
- *User task analysis and user training — thank you, Carol Feehan.*
- *Credit card integration — thank you, Jeff Harrison.*

- *Oracle alliance — thank you, Jeff Zimmerman.*
- *Humor and test scripts — thank you, Matt Melton.*
- *Merrill Lynch, the customer — thank you, John Creason and Phil Esparza.*
- *Merrill Lynch, the investor — thank you, Mark McAndrews and Heidi Evenson.*
- *The copy machine and events like this — thank you, Corkey Christianson.*
- *The mission statement, the Barn, and the Candles — thank you, Barbara Fagan.*
- *Press coverage and trade show booths — thank you, Jeanne Miller.*
- *MRDs, SRDs, and DDDs — thank you, Brad Stone.*
- *Salespeople, a marketing strategy, and our Baseline product definition — thank you, Katarina Bonde.*
- *Someone's ponytail to remind us of where we are in achieving our goal — thank you, Chris Bomberger.*
- *Workbench and an IntraNet strategy — thank you, Maurice Paige.*
- *Its license contracts and Series A documents*

— thank you, Jim Austin.

- *All the bridge loans — thank you, Silicon Valley Bank, Chanen, Painter, and Tim McMullen.*
- *Proper financial statements — thank you, Nancy Fletcher and Roger Clark.*
- *Direct deposit and bimonthly paychecks — thank you, Bob Colliton.*
- *Project schedules and Version 1.5 — thank you, Tom Bason.*
- *$25,000 in cash that was delivered in the nick of time — thank you, Scott Cawlfield.*
- *Quality recruiting — thank you, Janis Machala.*
- *Talented, experienced people to join our team — thank you to all of our newest employees for believing in the product, the people, and the possibilities.*

Of course, every individual has created many more stones in our mosaic than just those I have mentioned here, and together these stones have become an outstanding piece of art called Captura Software, Inc.

John Ruskin said, "The highest reward for a person's toil is not what they get from it, but what they become by it."

And what has Captura become?

- *Captura has become a successful, emerging growth company well on its way to market leadership.*
- *Captura has become a company that produces a "best-of-breed" software solution that Fortune 500 companies are buying.*
- *Captura has become a company that is generating a $3 million run-rate in its first revenue-producing year.*
- *Captura has become a company that people want to join because of its values and principles.*
- *Captura has become one of only two percent of the software companies in Seattle to be funded.*

And while these achievements alone are significant enough to acknowledge and to celebrate, I would also like to share with you what our future holds and what Captura will become in this next year.

- *Captura will become a company of more than 120 employees.*
- *Captura will become a company with an*

international presence.

- *Captura will become a financially strong company with revenues for the next twelve months exceeding $5 million.*
- *Captura will become the market leader in the T&E expense automation market and will single-handedly establish a brand new category in the software application market — intelligent workflow.*
- *And most importantly, Captura will remain a company committed to open communication, teamwork, personal/professional balance, passion, and fun!*

On each table, you will see a bottle of wine that is the end result of the efforts of the Captura off-site. Please raise a glass in a toast to our perseverance of our past, the reality of our present, and the promise of our future, and to fun along the way.

You must always remember to say "thank you" to your employees, to your customers, to your investors, and to the others who support your work as an entrepreneur. Between the dream and the realization of the dream lies a lot of work. It is hard and exciting and good work, but it is work. It requires your passion and your vision, but it also requires others who will believe in you and work with you. Thank them for their faith, for their trust, for their commitment. Only from a place of deep gratitude will you begin to reap the rewards of your special calling as an entrepreneur. Only from a place of humility will you truly be able to see the difference you have made in the world.

It is my wish that I may play some small part in influencing you to fulfill your unique potential. I hope this book has provided meaningful information for you to use in building your own business. It is my deeper desire, however, that it has also motivated and inspired you to keep pursuing your dreams, for there is nothing better than seeing dreams come true.

Notes

NOTES

EPILOGUE

IN THE YEAR since I gave that speech, Captura has reached and exceeded most of the objectives listed. It has been a year filled with new challenges and new learning (to appear in the next book). As this book goes to print, Captura has just been selected by the Ford Motor Company for a worldwide rollout of our product. It is every entrepreneur's dream to build a company that is the best at what it does. And it does not happen based on only one person's vision or efforts. In addition to the people mentioned in my speech, several others have joined my life in the past year to make a significant contribution to Captura and to me. So, I would like to take this opportunity to expand my list.

Where would Captura be without:

- The wisdom and guidance of other CEOs — thank you, Norman Nie and my TEC group.
- The expanded sales force — thank you, Jim Reverman.
- The new Fortune 500 customers — thank you, Alison Doucette, Bill Falk, and David Effgen.
- The contacts, the advice, the patience — thank you, Fred Harman.

- The Microsoft connection — thank you, Tony Audino.
- A strong and dedicated COO and the sports metaphors — thank you, Dan Vetras.
- A dedicated assistant to keep the CEO healthy and happy — thank you, Lynn Roodhouse.
- The many, many new employees who believe in my dream to build a different kind of company — thank you for your commitment and enthusiasm.